10 MINDFRAMES FOR LEADERS

10 MINDFRAMES FOR LEADERS

The **VISIBLE LEARNING**® Approach to School Success

Edited by **John Hattie** and **Raymond Smith**

CORWIN

FOR INFORMATION:

Corwin

A SAGE Company

2455 Teller Road

Thousand Oaks, California 91320

(800) 233-9936

www.corwin.com

SAGE Publications Ltd.

1 Oliver's Yard

55 City Road

London EC1Y 1SP

United Kingdom

SAGE Publications India Pvt. Ltd.

B 1/I 1 Mohan Cooperative Industrial Area

Mathura Road, New Delhi 110 044

India

SAGE Publications Asia-Pacific Pte. Ltd.

18 Cross Street #10-10/11/12

China Square Central

Singapore 048423

Acquisitions Editor: Ariel Curry

Associate Editor: Eliza B. Erickson

Editorial Assistant: Caroline Timmings

Production Editor: Tori Mirsadjadi

Copy Editor: Liann Lech

Typesetter: C&M Digitals (P) Ltd.

Proofreader: Barbara Coster

Indexer: Integra

Cover Designer: Gail Buschman

Marketing Manager: Deena Meyer

Printed in the United States of America.

Library of Congress Control Number: 2020909115

ISBN 978-1-0718-0013-3

This book is printed on acid-free paper.

SUSTAINABLE FORESTRY INITIATIVE

Certified Chain of Custody

Promoting Sustainable Forestry

www.sfiprogram.org

SFI-01268

20 21 22 23 24 10 9 8 7 6 5 4 3 2 1

Contents

About the Editors

Professor **John Hattie** is an award-winning education researcher and best-selling author with nearly 30 years of experience examining what works best in student learning and achievement. His research, better known as Visible Learning®, is a culmination of nearly 30 years synthesizing more than 1,600 meta-analyses comprising more than 90,000 studies involving over 300 million students around the world. John has presented and key-noted in over 350 international conferences and has received numerous recognitions for his contributions to education. His notable publications include *Visible Learning, Visible Learning for Teachers, Visible Learning and the Science of How We Learn*, and *Visible Learning for Mathematics, Grades K–12*.

Raymond Smith is an independent author consultant with Corwin, who partners with district and school leaders to grow their professional expertise. He is the coauthor of several books, including *Evaluating Instructional Leadership* (2015) and *Coaching for Instructional Leadership* (2018), as well as numerous Visible Learning® Resource Guides for professional development. Ray is a highly proficient professional developer specializing in high-impact leadership development, effective school-wide improvement practices, and leadership coaching. He is also a trained activator for Professor John Hattie's Visible Learning® change principles and practices.

About the Contributors

Janet Clinton is a professor of Evaluation and deputy dean of the Melbourne Graduate School of Education, and she is also the director of the Teacher and Teaching Effectiveness Research Hub at the University of Melbourne. She has wide national and international experience as an evaluator, educator, and author. Janet has worked in Australia, New Zealand, and the United States, and led over 120 national and international projects across multiple disciplines, in particular health and education. Her major interest in evaluation is the development of evaluation theory and methodologies. Her current evaluation work focuses on teacher and teaching effectiveness, models of implementation, as well as the use of evaluation as a vehicle for change management and building capacity.

Peter DeWitt runs competency-based workshops and provides keynotes nationally and internationally focusing on school leadership (collaborative cultures and instructional leadership) and fostering inclusive school climates. His work has been adopted at the state level and university level, and he works with numerous school districts, school boards, regional networks, and ministries of education in North America, Australia, Scandinavia, and the United Kingdom. Peter works as a school leadership coach in North America. He and his team of 10 leadership coaches focus specifically on instructional leadership. Additionally, he is a Visible Learning® Trainer working with John Hattie. The author of many books, Peter's latest publication is *Instructional Leadership: Creating Practice Out of Theory* (2020).

Jenni Donohoo is a researcher, educational consultant, and international keynote speaker. Jenni works with systems, school leaders, and teachers around the world to support high-quality professional learning. She is also the author of several bestselling books including *Quality Implementation* (2019), *Collective Efficacy* (2016), and *The Transformative Power of Collaborative Inquiry* (2016). Jenni has also published many peer-reviewed articles focused on collective teacher efficacy.

Douglas Fisher is a professor of Educational Leadership at San Diego State University and a leader at Health Sciences High and Middle College. He has served as a teacher, language development specialist, and administrator in public schools and nonprofit organizations. Doug has engaged in Professional Learning Communities for several decades, building teams that design and implement systems to impact teaching and learning. He has published numerous books on teaching and learning, such as the bestsellers *Developing Assessment-Capable Visible Learners* (2018) and *Engagement by Design* (2017).

Nancy Frey is a professor of Educational Leadership at San Diego State University and a leader at Health Sciences High and Middle College. She has been a special education teacher, reading specialist, and administrator in public schools. Nancy has engaged in Professional Learning Communities as a member and in designing schoolwide systems to improve teaching and learning for all students. She has published numerous books, including the bestsellers *The Teacher Clarity Playbook* (2018) and *Rigorous Reading* (2013).

Michael Fullan is co-leader of the New Pedagogies for Deep Learning global initiative. Recognized as a worldwide authority on educational reform, he advises policymakers and local leaders in helping to achieve the moral purpose of all children's learning. Michael received the Order of Canada in December 2012. He is a prolific, award-winning author whose books have been published in many languages. His recent publications, both from Corwin, are *Nuance* (2018) and (with Mary Jean Gallagher) *The Devil Is in the Details* (2020).

Zaretta Hammond is a national consultant and author of *Culturally Responsive Teaching and the Brain* (2015). Zaretta has published articles in *Educational Leadership*, *The Learning Professional*, and *Phi Delta Kappan*. She consults widely with school districts, regional education service agencies, and coaching organizations across the country on ways for leaders, coaches, and teachers to support students to accelerate their learning through culturally responsive education.

Jim Knight is a senior partner at the Instructional Coaching Group and director of the Kansas Coaching Project at the University of Kansas Center for Research on Learning. He has conducted more than two decades of research on instructional coaching and popularized the topic with his book *Instructional Coaching* (2007). Jim is the author of several bestselling books, including *The Impact Cycle* (2017) and *Better Conversations* (2015), and he has presented to more than 100,000 educators from six continents.

Laura Link is an assistant professor of Educational Leadership & Policy in the Urban Education department of the College of Public Service at the University of Houston Downtown. She has served in many K–12 central office and school-based leadership roles and has taught elementary, middle, high school, and college students throughout her 30 years of experience. Her research focuses on developing and supporting school leaders and organizational cultures that prioritize effective grading practices, collaboration, and meaningful assessment. She is the author of *Cornerstones of Strong Schools* (2007) and "Leadership for Grading Reform" in *What We Know About Grading* (2019) as well as the winner of several university community engagement awards. Laura presents nationally on the topics of high-impact leadership, K–12 grading, mastery learning, research-practice partnerships, and teacher support.

Sugata Mitra is a leading educational expert on the internet and children's learning. He is internationally known for his Hole-in-the-Wall experiment (1999) where he coined the term *minimally invasive education* (MIE). He is the recipient of many awards and honorary doctorates from India, the United Kingdom, and the United States, and was also the recipient of the first ever million-dollar TED Prize (2013). His groundbreaking work is featured in the Jerry Rothwell documentary *The School in the Cloud* (2018) and in his recently published book by the same name, *The School in the Cloud* (2019).

Dominique Smith is chief of educational services and teacher student support at Health Sciences High & Middle College. Dominique's major area of research and instruction focuses on restorative practices, classroom management, growth mindset, and the culture of achievement. In addition to his school leadership responsibilities, Dominique provides professional learning to K–12 teachers in groups large and small, on many topics that address classroom and school climate and organization. His publications include *The Teacher Credibility and Collective Efficacy Playbook* (2020), *All Learning Is Social and Emotional* (2018), and *Building Equity* (2017).

Dylan Wiliam is emeritus professor of Educational Assessment at UCL (University College London). In a varied career, he has taught in urban public schools, directed a large-scale testing program, and served in university administration in various roles, including dean of a School of Education and senior research director at the Educational Testing Service in Princeton, New Jersey. Over the last 20 years, Dylan's work has focused on supporting teachers all over the world to harness the power of assessment to support learning.

Introduction

How we think about the *impact* of what we do is more important than focusing on *what* we do

Practices Trump Labels and Beliefs Trump Practices

In the winter of 2008, Dr. Viviane Robinson, a professor of education at the University of Auckland, New Zealand, along with two of her colleagues, Claire Lloyd and Ken Rowe, released a study involving the impact of different leadership processes on student outcomes. They discovered, among other things, that school leaders' "impact on student outcomes will depend on the particular leadership practices in which they engage" (Robinson, Lloyd, & Rowe, 2008, p. 637). They identified five major dimensions of effective leaders: establishing goals and expectations; strategic resourcing; planning, coordinating, and evaluating teaching and the curriculum; promoting and participating in teacher learning and development; and ensuring an orderly and supportive environment. This finding caused Viviane and her colleagues to suggest that researchers and practitioners could elevate their attention from "a general focus on the impact of leadership, to examining and increasing the frequency and distribution of those practices that make larger positive differences to student outcomes" (pp. 637–638). Is it sufficient, however, to simply shift school leaders' focus to high-probability practices?

We think not. Clearly, school leaders don't have unlimited time, energy, and resources. Yes, they must have the basics of human relations, management, and financial acumen. So, as a matter of self-preservation, they have to figure out where their time, effort, and influence will count the most. They must decide where their leadership practice can make the biggest difference and have the greatest impact, and then deliberately set their course in that direction. So, yes, a focus on the higher-probability practices is a practical first step forward. However, by itself, it is insufficient. Why? Because a myopic focus on high-probability practices alone without an understanding of *why* school leaders are doing *what* they are doing and a focus on the

Effective school
leaders talk about
their mindframes
and their beliefs
and prove them
through their
practices and
results.

impact of what they did condemns them to a professional life in which they wander aimlessly from one innovation or influence to the next. Conversely, a vision without a *how* (i.e., high-probability practices) is the definition of daydreaming. Effective school leaders talk about their mindframes (i.e., ways of thinking) and their beliefs and prove them through their practices (i.e., the hows) and results (i.e., the what).

Just as school leaders' practices trump the labels under which school leaders operate, there is yet one more ordinal shift: school leaders' practices are trumped by the way school leaders think about their role. In other words, the way school leaders think about what they do is more important than what they do (the particular leadership practices)—hence their mindframes, or ways of thinking. Another way of saying this is, school leaders' beliefs and values, their mindframes, explain their actions and maximize their impact on teachers, parents, and students. What are these particular "ways of thinking," and how are they evidenced within school leaders? A major theme in this book is to explore the answers to these questions.

In the interim, imagine two school leaders each engaged in many of the same things—managing a facility, attending to human relations, conducting professional learning/meetings, engaging in classroom walkthroughs, and so on. The difference between these two school leaders can be found in how they process and relay how they think about the interpretations that matter. Consider the following example to help illustrate our point. As a school leader, Joel spends much time on ensuring everyone in the school knows, adopts, and promotes the goals and expectations they have jointly determined; gearing the strategic resources to realize these goals; and ensuring that the curriculum and teaching are constructed and evaluated to align with the goals. Emma, also a school leader, is more focused on the impact of her adults in the school (teachers, assistants, front office, support staff, librarians): that the adults have exemplars of what is meant by impact; that they know what a year's growth looks like; and that the notion of impact includes achievement, social and emotional aspects, and that programs are adapted when they are shown to not have sufficient impact on a sufficient number of students. She, too, ensures an orderly and supportive environment, promotes and resources teacher learning to maximize this impact, and continually questions whether the goals and expectations are appropriate. It is more than the right focus, it is the ways of thinking about these foci to ensure that they have the appropriate impact on the students in the school.

Simon Sinek and the Golden Circle

This idea—that one's thought about her or his impact of what they do precedes and guides their every action—is supported in the work of Simon Sinek (2009) and his thinking within his book *Start With Why: How Great Leaders Inspire Everyone to Take Action*. In this book, Sinek underscores the idea that "[i]t is not just WHAT or HOW you do things that matters; what matters more is that WHAT and HOW you do things is consistent with your WHY" (p. 166), which is why a focus solely on practices alone, even high-probability practices, represents an incomplete recipe for success. Successful leaders talk about their Why and prove it with what they do. The main question for these leaders is why something should be done. Answering this question leads them to the question of how to do something (e.g., high-probability practices) and finally to what, or the results of those actions. Sinek (2019) more recently noted that leaders are not responsible for the results; leaders are responsible for the people who are responsible for the results. "And the best way to drive performance in an organization is to create an environment in which information can flow freely, mistakes can be highlights and help can be offered and received. In short, an environment in which people feel safe among their own. This is the responsibility of a leader" (p. 129). We argue that leaders are responsible for demonstrating their thinking about the importance of results (we prefer impact, to avoid any narrow notion of only or merely increasing test scores—there are so many more important results than just test scores), for helping to ensure all have similar notions of what they are aiming to impact, and for the degree to which they are successful and want and need to be successful. Leaders should ensure that the resources needed for learning are provided for all to make the needed impact—and celebrating it when it occurs.

Consequently, the complete recipe for success is depicted in Figure i.1, what Sinek (2009) refers to as the "Golden Circle" (p. 37). Success has its origins in the inner

THE GOLDEN CIRCLE

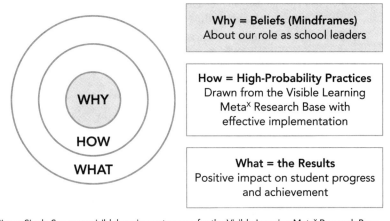

Why = Beliefs (Mindframes)
About our role as school leaders

How = High-Probability Practices
Drawn from the Visible Learning Meta^X Research Base with effective implementation

What = the Results
Positive impact on student progress and achievement

Source: Adapted from Simon Sinek. See www.visiblelearningmetax.com for the Visible Learning Meta^X Research Base.

Figure i.1

circle and the question of why and then radiates outward from there by school leaders asking the questions of how and what.

If we apply this simple yet powerful model to the ideas of mindframes and their relationship to Visible Learning®, then we would populate Sinek's (2009) Golden Circle with the following language. Mindframes are our Why. They represent an internal set of beliefs we hold near and dear to our hearts—a belief that our primary role is to be an evaluator of our impact on student learning, use assessment as a way to inform our impact and next steps, collaborate with our peers and students about that impact, be an agent of change, challenge others to not simply "do your best," give and help students and teachers understand feedback and interpret and act on the feedback given to us, engage in dialogue, inform others what successful impact looks like from the outset, build relationships and trust, and focus on learning and the language of learning. The Visible Learning+™ strategies and processes are the How to our Why. And the What refers to the result—the outcomes we intend to accomplish or the evidence of our collective impact on student progress and achievement.

So, what is your Why? As school leaders, each of us has an internal set of Whys that drives our external actions. The problem is, most of us have probably not sat down and clearly identified why we do what we do. And, if we have gone through that exercise, we most likely have not determined the degree to which our personal Whys are aligned with what the research says makes the greatest difference to the learning lives of students. And, how do your Whys align with the 10 mindframes for school leaders presented within this book? The Whys or mindframes reflect a summary of the 25+ years of Visible Learning research. The underlying theory of action for these 10 mindframes is ensuring school leaders have the expertise to communicate and act on their interpretation of the diagnosis of school and classroom data, selecting high-probability intervention(s), implementing these interventions effectively, and evaluating the impact of the selected interventions on student learning.

Ensuring School Leaders Have Expertise in Diagnosis, Interventions, Implementation, and Evaluation

If you are familiar with the Visible Learning® research, you will recall that the average effect size (i.e., the degree of impact of a particular influence on learning) of a year's progress is $d = 0.40$. And given the "flaws" of the average, this is but a broad benchmark needing a lot of contextual debates when applied in a school.

When the various education interventions we have reviewed in our Visible Learning work are considered, the most significant comes from teachers and school leaders, with many achieving a much greater effect than a year's growth for a year's input, as is illustrated by the following examples:

- Working together to evaluate their impact (0.93)

- Moving from what students know now toward explicit success criteria (0.77)

- Building trust and welcoming errors as opportunities to learn (0.72)

- Getting maximum feedback from others about their impact (0.72)

- Getting the proportions of surface to deep learning correct (0.71)

- Using the Goldilocks principles of challenge (not too hard, not too easy, and not too boring) (0.74)

- Using deliberate practice to attain these challenges (0.79)

To get these effects, however, requires listening to the learning happening in the schoolhouse (e.g., during classroom walkthroughs, professional learning sessions/meetings, professional learning communities) and classrooms. It requires less talk by teachers and school leaders and more listening to student and teacher dialogue; students talking to teachers about what it means to be a learner in their classes, and what they believe are the indicators of learning and progress; more evaluation of surface (content) and deep (relating and transferring content) teacher understanding and knowing when to move from one to the other; and leadership expertise that builds on a deep understanding of what teachers already know and can do relative to scaling high-probability instructional practices throughout the school.

The theory of action for such school leaders can be summed up by the phrase "School Leaders are to DIIE for!," that is, school leaders need to be expert at Diagnosis, Interventions, Implementation, and Evaluation. To be expert at diagnosis requires understanding how students and teachers are performing from multiple evidence-informed interventions so that if one does not work with the students and teachers, the school leader changes to another. It also involves knowing the interventions that have a high probability of success, knowing when to switch from one to another, and not using "blame" language to explain why students are not learning, as the problem of students not learning is more likely an adult not choosing the right teaching intervention rather than a student problem. To be expert at implementation requires a commitment to fidelity (i.e., adherence to the intervention curriculum); quality of delivery (i.e., the skill with which school leaders and/or facilitators deliver intervention material and interact with teachers); intervention adaptation (i.e., changes made to the intervention, particularly material that is added to the intervention); and dosage (i.e., the number of intervention professional learning sessions needed to efficiently and successfully implement the intervention). To be expert at evaluation requires knowing the skills of evaluating, having multiple methods, and working collaboratively and debating with colleagues to agree on the magnitude of the effect needed for an intervention to be successful. It requires what Clinton (Chapter 1) claims is a deep embedding in evaluative thinking.

The bottom line is, if students are not learning, then it is because we are not using the right teaching and/or school leader strategies; we have our expectations of success too low or far too high, and we have to make the necessary changes to these strategies to then realize our ambitious expectations. Such a theory of action places a number of demands on our teachers and school leaders, namely, that they begin with Why by communicating from the inside out; have a high level of cognitive decision-making skills that maintains a tight alignment between their Whys and how they do things and the results they achieve; are able and willing to say "I was wrong in my choice of a particular intervention and need to change what I do or say" or "I was right in my choice of interventions as they led to me successfully teaching these students"; and engage with others in collaborative inquiry about their diagnosis, interventions, implementation, and evaluation based on the evidence of their impact.

What is the VISIBLE LEARNING® Model?

The Visible Learning® school change model of professional learning is based on the principles that have developed from the Visible Learning research and two books—*Visible Learning* (Hattie, 2009) and *Visible Learning for Teachers* (Hattie, 2012)—as well as numerous articles and white papers. It takes the theory of this research and puts it into a practical inquiry model for schools to ask questions of themselves about the impact they are having on student achievement.

The Visible Learning research is based on John Hattie's meta-meta-analysis of more than 1,600 meta-analyses to date, composed of more than 90,000 studies involving more than 300 million students—possibly the world's largest evidence base to improve student learning. From that research, Hattie identified more than 270 factors that have an impact on student achievement. "Visible Learning seeks to get to the crux of this multitude of findings from educational research and identify the main messages by synthesizing meta-analyses. The aim is to move from 'what works' to 'what works best' and when, for whom, and why" (Hattie & Zierer, 2018, p. xviii). The 270+ (and growing) influences produced from the many meta-analyses have been assigned to one of nine domains: student, curricular, home, school, classroom, teacher, student learning strategies, instructional strategies, and implementation method. Then, each domain is further divided into subdomains—thirty-two in total in order to drill down into specific influences and the degree to which these influences accelerate student achievement.

How should educators use the Visible Learning research? The Visible Learning books serve as a *basis for discussion* on using evidence to inform your teaching and leadership practice, and the systems in which these practices are supported. One example might be the degree to which the school has developed a clear picture of the type of feedback culture and practice that they aspire to have. This can assist teachers to optimize their feedback and heighten students' awareness of the benefits of effective feedback. Similarly, it can help school leaders optimize their feedback and boost teachers' awareness of the benefits of feedback. Both of these actions serve to create an awareness of *how* feedback might be getting through to each of these key stakeholders.

Why This Book?

Over the past several years, it has been our privilege and pleasure to attend presentations or read books or articles by each of these authors whose work appears in this collection. As we listened and read, we were struck by the consistency of their message. Inasmuch as these authors had their own unique ways, as well as different ideas regarding the most effective strategies to produce a significant impact on the learning lives of students, their individual Whys for school leaders were remarkably similar. In addition, the concepts underlying their work kept returning to the same themes. They truly seemed to share a common belief about the way school leaders should view their role in order to bring about a year's worth of learning for a year's worth of teaching and leading.

We were convinced that school practitioners throughout the world who had the opportunity to explore the work of these experts would come to the same conclusion: There is coherence in their collective Why. We recognized, however, that most teachers and school leaders have neither the resources to attend professional conferences on a regular basis nor the time to devote to becoming students of the work of a variety of authors. Ultimately, we concluded that bringing the ideas of these educational thought leaders together into one book could be a tremendous resource for educators who are working to help their students achieve at ever-higher levels. We were thrilled when this outstanding collection of educational writers and thinkers agreed to contribute to the project.

It is important to note that each of these authors has had his or her own learning enriched and extended by observing the practices of exemplary schools and teachers and school leaders within them. These educators are truly school improvement leaders in their own right, and they represent a tremendous storehouse of collective wisdom. Thus, we hope this book will accomplish several objectives. First, we hope it will be a valuable tool for educators who are doing the hard work of improving their schools. We believe this collection offers them both a coherent conceptual framework and specific practical strategies for moving forward with their improvement efforts. The following table identifies, chapter by chapter, the author, the mindframe (i.e., the Why) the author is addressing, and the various high-probability influences (i.e., the How) the author has selected to illustrate strategies for bringing her or his identified mindframe to life.

Chapter	Author(s)	Mindframe	Influences Discussed
1	Janet Clinton	"I am an evaluator of my impact on teacher/ student learning"	1. Formative evaluation 2. Questioning
2	Dylan Wiliam	"I see assessment as informing my impact and next steps"	1. Mastery learning 2. Feedback 3. Collaborative learning (also discusses: • Self-regulated learning • Clear goal intentions)
3	Jenni Donohoo	"I collaborate with my peers and my teachers about my conceptions of progress and my impact"	1. Collective efficacy 2. Mastery learning 3. Appropriately challenging goals
4	Michael Fullan	"I am a change agent and believe all teachers/ students can improve"	1. Collaborative learning 2. Collective efficacy 3. Leadership
5	Zaretta Hammond	"I strive for challenge rather than merely 'doing my best'"	1. Teacher estimates of achievement 2. Collective efficacy 3. Formative evaluation
6	Peter M. DeWitt	"I give and help students/teachers understand feedback and I interpret and act on feedback given to me"	1. Teacher–student relationships 2. Teacher credibility 3. School leadership

Chapter	Author(s)	Mindframe	Influences Discussed
7	Douglas Fisher, Nancy Frey, and Dominique Smith	"I engage as much in dialogue as in monologue"	1. School climate 2. Collective efficacy 3. Microteaching
8	Laura Link	"I explicitly inform teachers/students what successful impact looks like from the outset"	1. Teacher clarity 2. Mastery learning 3. Formative evaluation
9	Sugata Mitra	"I build relationships and trust so that learning can occur in a place where it is safe to make mistakes and learn from others"	1. Questioning 2. Strong classroom cohesion 3. Collective efficacy
10	Jim Knight	"I focus on learning and the language of learning"	1. Formative assessment 2. Piagetian programs 3. Prior achievement

Second, we hope it will help bridge the gap that sometimes exists between researchers and practitioners. The intended audience for these authors is not other researchers, but teachers and school leaders who are engaged in the challenges of school reform on a daily basis. Each contributor has worked closely with schools; identified high-probability practices that, when implemented effectively, will have a positive impact on student learning; and now hopes to share his or her insights with educators throughout the world. As stated previously, each of our authors had their own unique ways, as well as different ideas regarding the most effective strategies to produce a significant impact on the learning lives of students. Toward that end, we note that this notion of authors' "unique ways" and "different ideas regarding strategies" raised a potential point of confusion for the reader that we wish to address prior to your reading of these chapters. The confusion appears in Chapters 1 and 10. Specifically, in Chapter 1, Professor Clinton prefers to use the phrase "formative and summative evaluation," while Dr. Knight, in Chapter 10, prefers the phrase "formative assessment." Inasmuch as we recognize and honor these two experts' personal preferences, for our purposes we view the two phrases as often being synonymous. When Michael Scriven (1967) invented the term, he never used the words *testing* or *assessment*—it was formative and summative evaluation. Moreover, when we are asked to explain the difference between formative and summative evaluation (e.g., assessment), we believe any evaluation (e.g., assessment) can be interpreted formatively or "summatively." As Robert Stake said, using a culinary metaphor, "When the cook tastes the soup, that's formative; when the guests taste the soup, that's summative" (Scriven, 1991a, p. 19). We note that too often, discussions using formative assessment rush too quickly to tests and measures, whereas it is more critical that school leaders use evidence (data, teacher and student voice, experience, artifacts of lessons, observations, etc.) to inform their thinking.

Finally, and perhaps most importantly, we hope that this book will convince school leaders that they should recognize, honor, and utilize the talent that is all around them, if we only had the courage to do so, and focus the narrative in schools around what is meant by impact, the Why to then inform the How. Our claim is that the greatest influence on student progress and learning is having highly expert, inspired, and passionate teachers and school leaders working together to maximize the effect of their teaching and leading on all students in their care. There is a major role for school leaders: to harness the expertise in their schools and to lead successful transformations.

"I AM AN EVALUATOR OF MY IMPACT ON TEACHER/STUDENT LEARNING"

Janet Clinton

My School Is Underperforming—What Can I Do?

Consider these two scenarios:

A school receives a notice from their district or regional leader that the school is underperforming academically in literacy, numeracy, and student engagement. The principal is asked to submit a school improvement plan as soon as possible. She sighs and considers options. She calls the leadership team together to discuss the directive. While some think the notice is strange, given that they thought things were getting better and they had been working so hard, the leadership team discusses the situation at the meeting and decides that direct action needs to be taken.

At the next staff meeting, the principal shares the directive and the discussion of the leadership team and then announces the following actions:

- There will be a change in the timetabling (e.g., master schedule) to accommodate more explicit teaching of numeracy and literacy.

- Class sizes will be reduced by three to four students in order to create one extra class in each grade.

- The whole school will engage in professional learning on the explicit teaching of numeracy and literacy across the grades.

(Continued)

(Continued)

- There will be a reduction in non-core-curricular activities such as sport, music, carnivals, and so on.

- Homework will only focus on numeracy and literacy practice.

- All teachers will be given access to the latest web platform featuring best practices on numeracy and literacy.

Although some staff express feeling a little shell-shocked, many think the actions should enhance academic scores. A few teachers wonder about student engagement and whether teaching will ever be fun again.

Across town, another school principal receives a similar directive. The principal decides to sleep on it because it doesn't make a lot of sense. The following morning the principal brings the leadership team together and asks whether they think the directive is correct. The leadership team feels the judgment about literacy and numeracy is correct, but the school has been on a strong growth trajectory and things are improving. Following some discussion, it is decided the team will explore perception and data in relation to numeracy and literacy levels in the school. The principal consults with the district office to explore their understanding a little more.

At the next staff meeting, the principal shares the directive and seeks a response from the staff. The staff explore ways of increasing the pace of the current work enhancing literacy and numeracy. The leadership team determines that the current growth trajectory is generally defensible, even though the school is still below the region's average academically. They also note that student and parent engagement appear to be just okay and need major improvement. The staff are not clear on what is happening across all the grades, but everyone knows Years 5 and 6 are a problem.

They agree on the following actions:

- The principal decides to hold a parents' evening focused on numeracy and literacy.

- The principal meets with the regional leader about the nature of the evidence, and the interpretations that led them to their conclusion.

- The leadership team decides to develop a monitoring plan about literacy, numeracy, and engagement and share the results with the district, and then implement it over the next two terms.

- Each alternative staff meeting becomes a sharing-of-ideas session instead of an administration meeting.

- Grades 3 and 4 teachers design a professional learning session with and for Grades 5 and 6 teachers.

- Grades 5 and 6 teachers run a numeracy and literacy capacity-building and knowledge evening for parents.

Questions to Consider

- What do these scenarios tell us about leadership actions? Which principal has the right approach? Which is demonstrating evaluative thinking with a focus on the impact on students? Which one reflects your school or a school you know?

- What outcomes would you predict for each school?

- Which school has a culture of considering the evidence and has built confidence for sharing?

- Consider what actions should be taken.

WHAT IS THIS CHAPTER ABOUT?

Thinking and acting evaluatively, questioning, and developing positive school cultures are core to Visible Learning®. This chapter explores the mindframe of the leader as evaluator. It explains the significance of evaluation leaders and how school leaders can build an evaluative culture in their schools. Consider the different responses to the two scenarios above. What will really make a sustainable and substantive difference?

There are three important notions in this mindframe: evaluator, impact, and learning. These notions go to the core of the act of teaching and learning and underpin all other nine mindframes. When teachers and school leaders have the disposition and the skills to evaluate their impact on students' learning, they will have the greatest impact. This way of thinking does not dictate any teaching methods, any program of work, or any leadership style. Instead, it highlights the capacity of educators to design effective programs informed by evidence, implement them with quality and fidelity, and then be able to critically determine the magnitude of the impact of their educational programs on student learning. It begs the moral purpose questions about what is meant across the school by impact, how many students experience this impact, and what the magnitude of the impact is. The role of the school leader is first to explain and develop an understanding in the school about these notions of impact and, second, to establish a school culture that supports active engagement in evaluation by ensuring time, resources, momentum, and expertise to allow a culture of evaluative thinking to flourish in the school.

The school leader's role is not merely to collect data, create reports, and "teach" teachers, but involves leading collaborative discussions about the nature and worth of the impact of programs on students and the interpretation of evidence about the impact of teaching. In doing this, school leaders must allow for multiple meanings and interpretations of evidence, impact, and teaching.

Acting and thinking evaluatively in this way requires supporting teachers to make judgments about their impact and seeking alternative views (i.e., valuing the second opinion, engaging in dialogue) about the credibility of their interpretations of this impact (triangulating with test scores, reviewing with colleagues, and listening to student interpretations of their own learning).

In essence we are pointing to the idea of building a learning organization where evaluative thinking is core and the key to success.

What Is Evaluative Thinking?

Evaluation refers to the process of determining the merit, worth, or significance of something, or the product of that process (Scriven, 1991b). We should not, however, confuse evaluative thinking with just doing evaluation. Evaluative thinking is a cognitive process; it is a way of being.

In education, it is a state of questioning, reflecting, making sound judgments, using good evidence, learning, modifying, and acting on maximizing impact on the learning lives of students as a matter of course. Baker and Bruner (2012) suggest that evaluative thinking "is an approach that fully integrates systematic questioning, data, and action into an organization's work practices" (p. 1). It builds on an organization's evaluation capacity to innovate and then to develop sustainability. Evaluative thinking is a cognitive process in the context of evaluation, "motivated by an attitude of inquisitiveness and a belief in the value of evidence, that involves skills such as identifying assumptions, posing thoughtful questions, pursuing deeper understanding through reflection and perspective taking and making informed decisions in preparation for action" (Archibald, Sharrock, Buckley, & Cook, 2016).

School Leaders Who Think Evaluatively

School leaders exhibiting evaluative thinking have greater pattern recognition, are more adept at checking their and others' assumptions, biases and constraints, are more able to monitor implementation of programs, and are more likely to seek alternative actions in the light of failure or resistance. Such school leaders are slower to come to problem representations and conclusions; they try to see the world through others' eyes, check back with the problem statement regularly, and overlearn the skills and views from the evaluating literature (theoretical and practical) to better integrate them and make more immediate and automatic selection in the moment by moment of school life.

WHICH FACTORS FROM THE VISIBLE LEARNING® RESEARCH SUPPORT THIS MINDFRAME?

An evaluative school leader is characterized as someone who is actively engaged in formative evaluation ($d = 0.34$), engaged in open questioning ($d = 0.48$), and able to create an evaluative school climate ($d = 0.43$).

Formative Evaluation

When Scriven (1967) first introduced the notion of formative and summative, he did so with respect to evaluation; however, other researchers morphed the concept into formative and summative *assessment*, which has led to many misleading claims. Here, we use the terms synonymously. Scriven argued that the distinction between formative and summative is more related to purpose and time, as illustrated by Robert Stake's maxim (cited in Scriven, 1991b): "When the cook tastes the soup, that's formative; when the guests taste the soup, that's summative" (p. 19). It is not the instrument (tasting) that is formative and summative; it is the timing of the interpretation and the purpose for which the information is used. A major role of the evaluative school leader is to make interpretations to improve the current status during the process of leading teaching and learning, and at appropriate summative moments—and at these summative moments to appropriately celebrate the success of teachers and motivate them to increase their positive impact on the learning lives of students. This notion of "learning lives" is quite broad and includes ensuring safety and fairness in the classroom, finding joy in the struggle and hard work of learning by teachers, endorsing multiple strategies of teaching learning, maximizing growth, and working with teachers to raise achievement in the lessons of the class.

As Scriven (1991b) has noted, it is a fallacy to assume that formative and summative represent two types of interpretations. Instead, they refer to interpretations of information at two differing times—interpretations that can lead to either changing a program of learning or a statement about the learning at the end of the program or intervention. In the same way that the goal of the cook is to make the best soup possible for the guests, it is imperative that school leaders have excellent summative evaluation in place in their school. Poor soup for the guests is pretty powerful evidence of poor cooking. If school leaders have poor summative assessment in place to support an overall evaluation, then it is unlikely they will have the ability, purpose, or where-withal to be concerned with formative interpretations. Serving poor soup to the guests is probably the best indicator that the cook was lousy at tasting it during the prepa-rations. Too much reliance on tasting the soup may lead to inattention to the goals, such as making the soup cold when the guests arrive. Thus, getting the balance right in the way school leaders implement formative and summative evaluations is critical.

Undertaking formative evaluation any less rigorously than summative evaluation undermines the accuracy of the mid-course corrections, which is all too likely to send the mission in the wrong direction. Contrary to popular utterance, it is the formative interpretations that need to be most rigorous; too often, mid-course cor-rections and evaluations about progress are based on very weak evidence, and there can be lower probability of attaining the goals of an intervention.

An aim should be to include evaluation in the planning, the doing, the continu-ously checking and monitoring, and in the review phases, as such interpretations can provide focus for intervention, information for adaptation, and evidence to continue or not with the program. A major purpose for school leaders is to lead and promote the interpretations. Ensure judgments are made while at the same time building the collective efficacy of the staff to engage in learning that is improved progressively in light of formative evaluations.

In the same manner, school leaders have responsibility for evaluating individual teachers in a manner where they receive feedback information to improve their impact on students. The effects of formative evaluation increase where there is an emphasis on interpretation from multiple sources of evidence, when school leaders have the necessary skills and mindframe to analyze and interpret data effectively (and with others), when there is attention to ensuring that the recipient of evalu-ative feedback correctly receives the interpretations, and when the quality of for-mative evaluation is judged by the degree to which improvement then occurs (see Harlen, 2007; Hendriks, Scheerens, & Sleegers, 2014; as well as other chapters in this volume). Formative evaluation requires capacity building within a school, ready access to multiple forms of evidence, a relentless focus on interpretations of this evidence, and a high sense of trust and climate of safety to explore successes and foci for improvement among the teachers and school leaders.

Questioning

Robinson (2009) has noted the power of school leaders engaging in "open-to-learning" conversations, which are "learning about the quality of the thinking and information that we use when making judgments about what is happening, why and what to do about it" (p. 1). This is key to evaluative thinking and is closely related to the ideal of formative evaluation. What distinguished these from closed conversations is not the focus of the conversation, but the openness to learning about others' points of view. This requires attention to questioning techniques, the ability to describe problematic situations and detect and challenge their own and others' assumptions and viewpoints, the skill of demonstrating to the other (teacher) that you have not only heard but understood (not necessarily agreed or disagreed), and the building of relational trust as the basis for enhancing the quality of what is happening across the school to successfully improve interventions and enhance the quality of learning for teachers and students in the school. A major essence of open-to-learning conversations is based on effective questioning.

We know that teachers are prolific questioners, asking 150–250 questions a day in their classes, mostly about the facts, and usually as a prompt for them to continue to the next part of the lesson. The research on optimal questions to enhance student learning, however, privileges those questions that elicit information for the teacher about what the students (plural and not just the question answerer) understand and particularly do not understand, such that the teacher modifies where they go next in their teaching. The questions need to be phrased in a manner that is understood by the students (which does not necessarily mean closed questions leading to "correct" answers); be preferably higher-cognitive-level questions; probe students' responses for clarification, support, and stimulation of thinking; and encourage students to respond in some way to each question asked (Redfield & Rousseau, 1981).

Nystrand, Wu, Gamoran, Zeiser, and Long (2003) also noted the power of "uptake" questions, when teachers effectively build on students' prior knowledge and current understandings by incorporating the students' responses into subsequent questions. Thus, the classroom discussion is less predictable (teacher question, student answer, teacher continues) and more a discourse or dialogue that is negotiated or co-constructed as teachers pick up on, elaborate, and question what students say (Nystrand, 1990; Nystrand & Gamoran, 1991). Such interactions, Nystrand (1990) argues, are also often characterized by "authentic" questions, which are "questions asked to obtain valued information, not simply to see what students know and don't know; authentic questions are questions without 'prespecified' answers" (pp. 6–7). The conversation is thus less pre-scripted and more open to learning, and the teacher can hear how many of the students are processing, engaging in, and reacting to the lesson.

These are the same characteristics of good questioning by school leaders: a focus on an openness to learn; privileging of those questions that elicit information for the school leader about what the teachers understand and particularly do not understand, such that the school leaders modify where they go next in their teaching; questions that are understood by teachers, probe for clarification, and support them; and uptake and authentic questions that invite and stimulate thinking and require a response.

There are five core evaluative thinking questions for school leaders (Table 1.1). The first is "What are students ready to learn?" In this case, we could change the word "students" to "teachers," which means that excellent diagnosis is needed to ensure that there is a triangulation of evidence about what is to be improved, the readiness of the teachers to engage in improvement, and an agreed focus on the diagnosis and improvement direction. The second is "Have I chosen optimal, evidence-based interventions and built a logic model to focus on implementation?" School leaders rarely lack in choice for intervention, and too many interventions are chosen because they are liked, are trialed by the school leader elsewhere, or involve the least disruption. But do they fit the diagnosis, is there a plan to appropriately adapt to the local situation, and is there an up-front process to

THE FIVE EVALUATIVE QUESTIONS RELATING TO EVALUATIVE THINKING

Evaluative Thinking	Evaluative Questions
1. Critical thinking valuing evidence	1. What are students ready to learn?
2. Addressing the fidelity of implementation	2. Have I chosen optimal, evidence-based interventions and built a logic model to focus on implementation?
3. Investigating potential biases	3. Am I seeking evidence that I might be wrong?
4. Focusing on knowing one's impact	4. What are the shorter-, medium-, and longer-term impacts expected, and am I monitoring and reporting these?
5. Understanding others' points of view	5. Am I seeking others' perspectives and evidence about fidelity and impact?

Table 1.1

monitor implementation to ensure the highest chance of attaining agreed (short-, medium-, and long-term) goals?

The third question is "Am I seeking evidence that I might be wrong?" This is core to being open-minded and an essential skill in school leaders' open-to-learn conversations. Hattie and Zierer (2018) make much of this question as core to Visible Learning®, and it derives from the philosophical claims by Popper (1959), who argued that falsification was the major difference between science and belief. Seeking evidence that one might be wrong entails seeking feedback about what is working and what is not working, and the degree to which the intervention is having an effect, and it is more likely to lead to improvements. The alternative, seeking information only about what is working, is often the source of confirmation bias, as there is always some evidence, somewhere, with some teachers that "it" is working. However, the intervention might have been working anyway regardless of any school leader impact. It might mask critical avenues for improvement, and it might lead to continuing with a program that eventually will show little impact.

The fourth question is "What are the shorter-, medium-, and longer-term impacts expected, and am I monitoring and reporting these?" This is a question typically associated with building program logics (Funnell, 2000), and it allows for immediate seeking of feedback to ensure that the program is going in the right direction. More often, the shorter-term impacts are proxies or indicators of implementation (was the program implemented with appropriate fidelity, dosage, adaptability, and quality?), and the too-early focus is on the longer-term impacts (changes to student learning and achievement). Thus, programs can be abandoned or changed in directions that do not subsequently lead to these improvements. School leaders who work with their teachers to be clear and agreed on the short-, medium-, and long-term impacts are more likely to engender feedback for improvement, appropriately adapt the program to local conditions, and achieve the desired impacts.

The fifth question is "Am I seeking others' perspectives and evidence about fidelity and impact?" As noted in Robinson's claims above, this requires particular skills to not only listen to the teachers, and show the teachers that you have listened, but to then use the empathy to collectively work toward the goals of the program and school. Woolley, Chabris, Pentland, Hashmi, and Malone (2010) have shown this question to be necessary for the "wisdom of the crowd" and for collective efficacy to be realized. Note that this sensitivity to others is related not merely to building group cohesion and goodwill but also to attending to the fidelity of program implementation and maximizing agreed-upon outcomes.

School Culture

Schools with a culture in which everyone is responsible for the progress of the students, schools that deprivatize the information and evidence, and schools that collaborate to improve learning are great schools (Hattie, 2012; Hattie & Timperley, 2007). Building a learning culture and a system for continuous reflection is key, and thinking evaluatively is essential. When did you meet with colleagues and talk about the evidence of progress of your and their students, how to improve your teaching, how to enhance your teaching, and how to do this in light of the evidence that what you are currently doing is just not good enough to have the effect on progress of students? Do you feel psychologically safe to discuss how to improve your teaching (not talking about the students, not the curriculum, not the resources, not the class size, not the conditions, but the impact of teaching of your staff) and leading? (To be clear, it is not discussing how we teach or lead, but the impact of this teaching and leading, which then may relate to the How). Such school leaders built assessment-rich schools (using test scores, evidence from assignments and projects, artifacts of student work, and student voice about their learning), and the teachers are mirroring the same classroom climate with their students—let's learn together and respect each other by seeking evidence that we can improve and are doing a great job. The desired climate is where teachers and school leaders share their interpretations about assessment, students, and teaching.

School culture is about "how we work here in this school"; can relate to a shared sense of purpose; defines and routinely monitors the norms of collegiality, improvement, and hard work; involves rituals and traditions to celebrate success; and most often provides an informal network of storytellers and a web of information. Marzano, Gaddy, Foseid, Foseid, and Marzano (2005) found that the most common behaviors of effective school culture are promoting cohesion, well-being, and an understanding of purpose among the staff, and developing a shared vision of what the school could be like.

The meta-analysis by Bulris (2009) was based on thirty studies and included over 3,000 schools. The overall correlation between school culture and achievement was $r = 0.35$ (converts to $d = 0.74$), which is substantial. He concluded that school leaders need to attend to the cultural elements within their school, school culture should be a key part of the evaluation of school leaders, and "establishing a school culture supportive of continuous improvement is the only way to provide opportunities for lasting and sustainable school improvement to occur" (p. 167).

WHERE CAN I START?

A number of strategies are germane to developing evaluative thinking in schools, and there are some necessary conditions that provide the climate for change. The identified preconditions do not operate in isolation and extensively affect each other. For instance, relational trust between teachers and school leaders supports the development of a positive school climate. Other strategies might include the following:

Create a climate of shared questioning

- Create a safe space for speculation
- Talk about and learn from the failures
- Challenge the generalizations and explore the contradictions
- Ensure learning occurs as we go
- Ask "So what?" and "What next?"

Promote active engagement in evaluation

- Use backward mapping—where do we want to get to and how will we get there?
- Take action—use logic models and evidence platforms
- Engage in a collaborative cycle of exploration
- Emphasize sense making

Provide resource systems to review data

- Triangulate the evidence
- Mobilize the data on effective practice
- Follow the path but be aware of the forks in the road
- Use a learning management system

Focus on feedback for all

- Provide opportunity for feedback to build upon
- Ensure coaches are focusing on data
- Promote what comes next from data reviews

The focus of the evaluative thinking, in the context of schools, always has learning at its core. Aligned to this is how school leaders impact the learning by teachers and students. Illeris (2015) argued that learning involves an interaction between a learner and the environment and evokes an internal acquisition process that includes the learning content and the learning incentive. The content of learning can include many pertinent aspects: knowledge, skills, attitudes, understandings, beliefs, behavior, and competencies.

The incentive is the investment of mental energy to drive the learning, to develop a mental model of inquiry that relates to learning. School leaders need to have clarity on the desired and required content, engender investment to drive teacher learning, and understand barriers and enablers of this learning (see Hattie & Donoghue, 2016).

Maximizing the process of analysis and ensuring an openness of their evaluative judgments about learning requires school leaders to deeply know, understand, and respect their teachers' and their own needs. This might include taking into account their prior learning, understanding how teachers use learning strategies to enhance their teaching, being explicit with teachers about what success looks like near the start of a series of school-wide interventions, implementing high-probability impact programs that have the optimal proportion of emphasis on surface and deep learning, and having appropriate levels of challenge—never accepting "do your best."

CHECKLIST

Working and thinking evaluatively means

☐ understanding that evaluation is action and evaluative thinking is a way of being,

☐ creating an environment where evaluation is not a threat but a desired activity,

☐ resourcing engagement in evaluative and data-gathering activities,

☐ modeling a questioning mindset, and

☐ having a plan for formative evaluation in your school.

EXERCISES

1. Bring together the leadership review learning outcomes in the school and map all the possible explanations for the results focus. Consider the factors you have control over and the ones you don't. Consider the evidence you have or do not have for the factors you have control over. Brainstorm what can be done about it.

2. Create groups to collate and display all the data about a specific question in your school. Ask the school staff to interpret it and consider what's next.

3. Ask the staff about their evaluation needs.

"I SEE ASSESSMENT AS INFORMING MY IMPACT AND NEXT STEPS"

Dylan Wiliam

Jacki—a science teacher with over twenty years of experience—is teaching a Year 8 science class about types of levers. She has explained to the class that, in classifying levers, what matters is the relative position of fulcrum, resistance, and effort, which means there are three different kinds of levers:

1. The fulcrum is between the load and the effort (see-saw).

2. The resistance is between the fulcrum and the effort (nutcracker).

3. The effort is between the fulcrum and the load (tweezers).

The class seems to be understanding. She can't see any students frowning, and when she asks the class if anyone has any questions, no one raises their hand.

She is aware that students may not be asking questions because they do not want to appear foolish, so she probes the class's understanding by asking the class about other kinds of levers to see if the students can correctly classify them. She asks the class what kind of lever a shoehorn would be. A dozen students raise their hands. She calls on one of them, who says that a shoehorn is a type 1 lever. She asks the rest of the class if they agree, and as far as she can tell, all the students nod. She then asks about a stapler, and again, about a dozen students raise their hands. She chooses one student, who correctly identifies a stapler as an example of a type 3 lever, and, when asked, again all the students agree that this is correct. She then asks about a wheelbarrow. This time, she asks students to call out their answers in unison, and as far as she can tell, all students shout out, "Two."

Satisfied that the class has understood the principles she is teaching, Jacki is about to move on, but, just to be sure, she asks the class what kind of lever a pair of pliers would be. She has been involved with a research project investigating classroom formative assessment, so, rather than selecting individual students for an answer, she asks each student to hold up one, two, or three fingers to indicate their choice. She is surprised to see that well over half the class thinks that a pair of pliers is a type 2 lever. After the lesson, Jacki is visibly shaken by the experience. She has taught this lesson dozens of times, and she has always assumed that the evidence she has been getting from her classroom questioning has been a good indication of the class's understanding. She has just discovered that it is not.

WHAT IS THIS CHAPTER ABOUT?

This chapter is premised on a simple idea: teachers and school leaders will make better decisions if they have better evidence of what is happening in their students' and teachers' heads. In 1968, American psychologist David Ausubel wrote the following in the introduction to his book on educational psychology: "If I had to reduce all of educational psychology to just one principle, I would say this: The most important single factor influencing learning is what the learner already knows. Ascertain this and teach him accordingly" (Ausubel, 1968, p. vi). For much of the past two-and-a-half millennia, this was easy advice to follow, because most education involved a single student and a single teacher. Teaching was engaging, because the teacher focused all his or her attention on the student, and it was responsive, in that the teacher constantly adjusted what he or she was doing in the light of what the student knew.

However, beginning in the middle of the seventeenth century, when communities around the world began to establish formal schools, the nature of education changed. Education changed from being a largely individual, personalized process to a form of "mass production" in which students were taught in batches. There can be little doubt that when teaching large groups, teachers cannot be as responsive to the needs of individual students, and students tend to be less engaged. This chapter focuses on how we can use classroom formative assessment to make the teaching of large, diverse groups of students—which are, after all, the norm in most education systems—more like one-to-one tutoring. In other words, to make teaching more engaging for students, and more responsive to their needs.

> Teachers and school leaders will make better decisions if they have better evidence of what is happening in their students' and teachers' heads.

WHICH STRATEGIES FROM THE VISIBLE LEARNING® RESEARCH SUPPORT THIS MINDFRAME?

Although formative evaluation is listed in its own right as a Visible Learning® influence, classroom formative assessment—focusing specifically on minute-to-minute and day-by-day assessment processes—draws together a number of other Visible Learning strategies.

Mastery Learning

The first strategy is Benjamin Bloom's work on mastery learning, which, building on John B. Carroll's view of aptitude as the time taken to learn something, assumed that most (i.e., 95 percent) students could learn anything if given enough time. Rather than teaching something once and accepting that some students would learn it and others would not, the key idea of mastery learning was the use of assessment to determine what students had learned and, if necessary, to do something about it. For Bloom, the traditional "bell curve" of results was a sign of educational failure: "In fact, we may even insist that our educational efforts have been unsuccessful to the extent to which our distribution of achievement approximates the normal distribution" (Bloom, 1968, p. 3).

The reasons that some students learn more than others from the same teaching are complex. We have known for years (indeed, centuries) that students differ in their motivation for learning, but recent work, such as John Sweller's work on Cognitive Load Theory, has shown that students can successfully complete the instructional tasks they are assigned, with no change in long-term capability—students do not necessarily learn what they are taught, even when that teaching appears to have been successful. And yet, as David Ausubel pointed out over 50 years ago, one of the most important principles of effective instruction is that we start from where the learner is, rather than where we might wish they were. For instruction to be effective, we have to first find out where learners are in their learning. Now, of course, teachers have always used what Madeline Hunter called "checks for understanding," but in many, and perhaps most, classrooms, this involves checking on the understanding of the students who are willing to raise their hands and volunteer responses. Effective teaching is possible only if teachers are collecting evidence frequently from all, or at least most, of the students in the class, and then using that information to adjust what they are doing to better meet students' learning needs. In other words, from a mastery learning perspective, teaching is no longer a linear but a *contingent* process. This can, of course, be seen as a form of feedback—from the learners to the teacher—but in terms of the focus of this chapter, it seems more helpful to use the term *feedback* for the information from teachers to learners.

Feedback

The second strategy that supports this mindframe is feedback. As well as collecting evidence on what learners are learning, teachers need to use this information to adjust their own instruction and to provide information to learners about what they need to do to improve. In looking at research on feedback, it is important to note that most feedback research—Ruiz-Primo and Li (2013) estimate 75 percent—is conducted in university psychology laboratories, on undergraduate students, and in most cases feedback is a single event lasting minutes. It is obviously unclear whether such research would generalize to primary and secondary school class-rooms, where teachers have continuing relationships with their students. More importantly, as Kluger and DeNisi (1996) point out in their meta-analysis of feedback research, whether feedback improves achievement—and if so, by how much—is less important than the kinds of responses made by recipients. After all, if feedback improves performance, but does so by making the learner more dependent on the feedback, or if the effects are transitory, this is unlikely to be helpful. The quality of the feedback is far less important than what students do with it, and, as every teacher knows, the same feedback may spur one student to increased effort but cause a similar student to give up. Teachers need to know their students—when to push and when to back off—and students need to trust teachers: if students do not believe that their teachers know what they are talking about, or do not think the teachers have the students' best interests at heart, then students are unlikely to invest the time needed to assimilate the feedback. This, in turn, highlights the importance of a growth mindset, not as an end in itself, but as a means to an end. To the student with a fixed mindset, feedback is unwelcome, because it may show that the student is not as intelligent as she or he thinks; for the student with a growth mindset, feedback is welcome, because it provides the student with advice about the best way to become more intelligent.

Collaborative Learning

The third area of research is the now extensive evidence on collaborative and coop-erative learning. While the research shows that having students work together can produce substantial increases in student achievement, these benefits occur only when students are working *as* a group rather than *in* a group (i.e., they are all working toward the same goal) and when each member of the group is individually account-able to the group for making their best effort, with each member of the group able to determine the efforts being made by others (Slavin, Hurley, & Chamberlain, 2003). What this means is that when teachers use cooperative or collaborative learning as part of their classroom routines, the teacher is still responsible for making sure that the support that students provide each other is accurate and helpful.

One particularly important aspect of collaborative learning is the use of peer assess-ment. While much of the research on peer assessment, particularly that in higher education, focuses on whether students are able to assess peers' work with the same accuracy as teachers, for primary and secondary school students, peer assessment is generally more helpful if it is focused on improving, rather than evaluating, work. Peer assessment—first assessing the work of anonymous peers, and then actual peers—can help learners internalize the success criteria for an instructional task, and they can do so in a setting that is less emotionally charged than assessing one's own work. When students have learned what it means to be successful on a task by looking at the work of others, they are more likely to be able to apply those criteria to their own work (see section on Clear Goal Intentions below).

Self-Regulated Learning

The fourth area of research that bears on classroom formative assessment concerns students becoming better at managing their own learning, through the use of meta-cognition (thinking about thinking) and what psychologists call "self-regulated learning" (getting students to have greater ownership of their own learning). While different psychologists use slightly different definitions (and self-regulated learning and metacognition are listed as different Visible Learning strategies), there does seem to be broad agreement among psychologists that there are three important compo-nents in this area: cognition (thinking), metacognition (thinking about thinking), and motivation (again listed as a separate strategy). Indeed, self-regulated learning can be seen as the goal of all the other strategies. When students (or teachers!) ask "How did I do?" one powerful response is "How do you think you did?" If the student (or teacher) can correctly identify what aspects need improving, then they are able to give feedback to themselves. Feedback that provides students with step-by-step guid-ance on what to do to improve a piece of work may well improve the work, but it is likely to have little benefit for the student because all the thinking has been done by the teacher. The main aim of feedback is to improve the student, not the work. It is to help the student do better, at some point in the future, on a task they have not yet attempted. Indeed, a major goal of effective feedback is to work toward its own redun-dancy. Good feedback helps learners be less dependent on feedback in the future.

> When students (or teachers!) ask "How did I do?" one powerful response is "How do you think you did?"

Clear Goal Intentions

The final strategy that is relevant for classroom formative assessment is that of teachers having clear intentions about what their students are to learn (clear goal intentions). Whether, and at what point in their instruction, teachers share those learning intentions with their students is a matter of some debate and, ultimately, probably a matter of professional judgment. However, there can be little doubt that teaching is likely to be more effective if the teacher is clear about the changes in students' knowledge, understanding, or capabilities that they hope will result from their teaching, rather than just engaging their students in a series of interest-ing and engaging classroom tasks.

STRATEGIES OF
FORMATIVE ASSESSMENT

	Where the learner is going	Where the learner is now	How to get there
Teacher	Clarifying, sharing, and understanding learning intentions and success criteria	Engineering effective discussions, tasks, and activities that elicit evidence of learning	Providing feedback that moves learning forward
Peer		Activating students as learning resources for one another	
Learner		Activating students as owners of their own learning	

Source: Leahy et al. (2005).

Figure 2.1

It is also important to note that it is useful to distinguish between learning intentions and success criteria. The learning intention is the increase in capability that the teacher hopes will result from engaging in the instructional tasks that he or she organizes for the students. However, since learning is a change in long-term memory, it is impossible to determine whether learning has taken place in a lesson. That is where success criteria come in. Success criteria are statements of what will happen if the instructional activity has gone as planned—a sort of "I'll be happy if" statement—so that the teacher can judge whether to move on or not. In terms of the psychological jargon, learning intentions are descriptions of the *learning* that it is hoped will take place as a result of engaging in the instructional tasks specified by the teacher, while success criteria are descriptions of the *performance* on those tasks.

The way that Leahy, Lyon, Thompson, and Wiliam (2005) found most useful for presenting these five strategies to teachers is in the form of the diagram shown in Figure 2.1.

What Is the Evidence That These Strategies Improve Student Achievement?

As noted above, there is considerable evidence that each of these strategies can positively impact student learning. In recent years, however, there have been a number of studies exploring the impact of these strategies when implemented collectively.

A meta-analysis of formative assessment interventions by Kingston and Nash (2011, 2015) found an average effect size of 0.2. This may seem like a modest effect, but all of the studies included in the review involved secondary school students and involved interventions that lasted at least a semester (and in most cases, a whole year), with student achievement being measured with standardized tests and the effect size quoted being the *additional* progress compared with "business as usual." With such assessments, one year's learning for ten-year-olds is around 0.4 standard deviations, and across all students of secondary school age, the average is 0.3 (Bloom, Hill, Black, & Lipsey, 2008). An increase of 0.2 standard deviations therefore represents an increase in the rate of learning of 50 percent to 70 percent—a dramatic improvement in student learning.

To test the effectiveness of formative assessment at scale, the UK Education Endowment Foundation commissioned a two-year, randomized-control evaluation of the "Embedding Formative Assessment" (EFA) program (Leahy & Wiliam, 2009). Half of a sample of 140 secondary schools in England were given access to the program materials, and half of the schools received the cash equivalent (£295, or about A$500).

The program introduces teachers to the five strategies of classroom formative assessment shown in Figure 2.1 and asks each teacher to select one or two practical techniques they would like to try out, such as selecting students at random, providing feedback in the form of comments rather than scores or grades, and so on. The teachers then meet monthly in groups of eight to twelve, where they discuss their experiences over the previous month and then make commitments about what they are going to do over the coming month to further develop their practice of classroom formative assessment. The EFA program provides a set of agendas and handouts for each meeting, including specific guidance for the teachers who are leading each group.

Teachers in the participating schools were encouraged to use formative assessment with all the classes they taught, but the focus of the evaluation was on students who began their final two years of compulsory schooling (Year 10 and Year 11) in September 2015. The outcome measure was the grades achieved by these students in their school-leaving examinations taken in May and June 2017.

Students in schools assigned to the EFA program scored 0.13 standard deviations higher on their national school-leaving examinations than those in the comparison schools at the end of the two-year program (Speckesser et al., 2018). Since one year's progress for students of this age is approximately 0.3 standard deviations, and making adjustments for summer learning loss and the fact that the school-leaving exams take place well before the end of Year 11, then an increase of 0.13 standard deviations over a two-year period equates to a 25 percent increase in the rate of learning. Given that the estimated cost of the program is £1.20 (A$2.00) per student per year, the EFA program is one of the most cost-effective ways of improving student achievement currently available. Put bluntly, any leader who is serious about raising student achievement needs to make classroom formative assessment a priority for their school.

The first decision that school leaders need to make is whether to involve all teachers from the outset or begin with a smaller group that is especially keen to develop this aspect of their practice. There are arguments for both, but in Leahy et al.'s (2005) work with schools around the world, they generally found that starting with "volunteers" rather than "conscripts" is better, as it allows schools to create some success stories and also to find what kinds of adjustments need to be made to make classroom formative assessment work in a particular setting.

Teachers then need to be introduced to some basic techniques of formative assessment—my advice would be between ten and twenty—either by reading articles or watching videos, and then asking each teacher to choose one or two techniques to try out in their classrooms. School leaders often want to get all the teachers working on the same technique, but adoption is far better when teachers choose for themselves which techniques to try out.

Next, teachers should be organized into groups—ideally with ten to twelve members in each group—and they should meet monthly to support each other and get new ideas (Jenni Donohoo addresses the impact of the high-probability practice of collective efficacy in Chapter 3). Although each group can decide the agenda for these meetings, in Leahy et al.'s (2005) work with teachers around the world, they saw considerable benefits from adopting a standard structure for the monthly meetings. The fact that each meeting follows the same structure means that participants come to the meeting knowing the roles they are to play, in terms of both reporting back on their own experiences and providing support to others. Over the years, Leahy et al. (2005) explored a number of possible different models, but the model presented below has worked well in all the different settings in which it has been tried.

Monthly Meeting Model
Introduction (5 minutes)

Agendas for the meeting are circulated and the learning intentions for the meeting are presented.

Starter activity (5 minutes)

Participants engage in a "warm-up" activity to help them focus on their own learning.

Feedback (25 minutes)

Each teacher gives a brief report on what they committed to try out at the previous meeting, while the rest of the group listens appreciatively and then offers support to the individual in taking their plan forward.

New learning about formative assessment (25 minutes)

In order to provide an element of novelty and a steady stream of new ideas, each meeting includes an activity that introduces some new ideas about formative assessment. This might be a task, a video to watch and discuss, or a book study in which teachers discuss a book chapter relevant to formative assessment that they have read over the past month.

Personal action planning (15 minutes)

The penultimate activity of each session involves each of the participants planning in detail what they hope to accomplish before the next meeting. This may include trying out new ideas, or it may simply be to consolidate techniques with which they have already experimented. This is also a good time for participants to plan any peer observations that they want to undertake.

Summary of learning (5 minutes)

In the last five minutes of the meeting, the group discusses whether they have achieved the learning intentions they set for themselves at the beginning of the meeting. If they have not, there is time for the group to decide what to do about it.

The Role of Leaders

One particularly important finding from Leahy et al.'s (2005) work with schools around the world is that these meetings are more successful if membership is restricted to those who are still teaching, which is why we call these groups *teacher learning communities*—a teacher learning community (TLC) is a special kind of professional learning community where full membership is restricted to those who are still teaching. School leaders will, of course, want to keep a finger on the pulse of what is happening at these meetings, but typically, the presence of senior staff, especially if they are no longer teaching, always changes the group's behavior, no matter how inclusive the leader tries to be. The crucial thing about a TLC is that there are no experts, just like-minded professionals meeting together to support each other in their professional development.

Of course, school leaders do need to monitor the progress of the TLCs, but the best way to do that is for school leaders to meet with the TLC leaders regularly (once every month or two). This will provide leaders with all the information they need about how the TLCs are doing, as well as providing support for the TLC leaders—the school leader becomes, in effect, the leader of a professional learning community of TLC leaders.

How will we know it's working?

Although the goal of any attempt at school improvement is, ultimately, improvement in student outcomes, these can often take some time to materialize—some schools have seen improvement in student achievement within a year, but it is more common for significant impact on student achievement to take two years. Where schools are under pressure to increase student achievement, two years can seem like a long time to wait to see if the school is on the right track. For this reason, Leahy et al. (2005) prepared a checklist of things that will be happening in classrooms if things are working well.

- ☐ Teachers are provided professional development in effective teamwork skills, given time to meet in TLCs, and do so.

- ☐ Teachers increasingly act as "critical friends" to others.

- ☐ The prevalence of well-implemented classroom formative assessment practices observed in "learning walks" is increasing.

- ☐ Students are more engaged in classrooms.

- ☐ Teachers modify the techniques in appropriate ways, indicating an understanding of the underlying theory.

- ☐ There is a shift in the ownership of the reform, with teachers taking increased responsibility for the content of meetings.

Conclusion

The basic idea of formative assessment—that teachers and leaders will make better instructional and leadership decisions if they have better evidence about what is happening in their students' and teachers' heads—is so obvious that it hardly seems worth mentioning. Assessment really is the bridge between teaching, leading, and learning: it is only by assessing our students and teachers that we can determine whether the educational strategies in which our students have engaged have resulted in the desired learning. And yet around the world, teachers continue to make decisions about what to do next in their teaching based on evidence from a few confident, articulate students. Once teachers realize that students' facial expressions and self-reports are not particularly useful guides to what is happening inside their heads, it is our experience that teachers quickly embrace the power of formative assessment and understand the value of focusing less on what they are putting into the educational process, and more on what students are getting out of it.

There are, of course, many other things that schools can do to improve student achievement, but it seems, given the very positive cost-benefit ratio described earlier, that attention to classroom formative assessment must be part of any school's plan to improve student achievement. As long as teachers and leaders are asking "What did I do?" and "What did my students learn?" and exploring the relationship between these two, then they will always be able to improve their practice.

"I COLLABORATE WITH MY PEERS AND MY TEACHERS ABOUT MY CONCEPTIONS OF PROGRESS AND MY IMPACT"

Jenni Donohoo

Cirque du Soleil originated with only twenty street performers in 1984 and has since grown into an organization that reinvented circus acts. In the past 36 years, Cirque du Soleil has performed in 450 cities in sixty countries and now employs 4,000 people. What is the leadership philosophy behind their success? Leaders strive to ignite creativity through risk-taking and tapping into the powerful force of positive interdependence. In *The Spark: Igniting the Creative Fire That Lives Within Us All*, the former president of Cirque du Soleil's Creative Content Division shares key ideas about how the Cirque du Soleil community thinks about its collaborative work. These include identifying challenging goals, mastering larger routines through incremental practice and feedback, and learning together about how to get better at connecting with and touching people in new ways. Readers who have attended a Cirque du Soleil show and witnessed the coordinated acrobatics will understand how all members of the community count on each other (with their lives) to produce a collective impact.

WHAT IS THIS CHAPTER ABOUT?

In Hattie and Zierer's (2018) book, *10 Mindframes for Visible Learning: Teaching for Success,* this mindframe—"I collaborate with my peers and my teachers about my conceptions of progress and my impact"—is about *teachers* believing in the importance of shared responsibility, collaboration, and consolidation of strengths as a team. This chapter considers this mindframe from a leadership perspective and outlines why valuing collaboration in relation to progress and impact is not only important to teachers' success but also a critical attribute of successful leadership.

The vignette illustrates this chapter's main message: reinventing teaching, leading, and learning requires that educators learn together in a community that shares common goals and understands the value of positive interdependence. Leaders help teams in mastering tasks required for improvement by providing feedback and adequate time for professional learning. Like the leaders in the Cirque du Soleil community, school and system leaders understand the importance of monitoring progress and knowing their collective impact.

On completion of this chapter, you will be able to take this message as a basis for explaining

- the significance of the factors "collective efficacy," "mastery learning," and "appropriately challenging goals";
- ways to focus collaboration on instructional improvement; and
- why goal setting is important and how it works.

WHICH FACTORS FROM THE VISIBLE LEARNING® RESEARCH SUPPORT THIS MINDFRAME?

There are many school leaders who collaborate regularly with their peers both formally and informally. It would be wrong to suggest that school and system leaders do not work together for the common goal of improving schooling. What is unfortunate, however, is when cooperation among principals and/or district leaders is artificially contrived, is undervalued, or lacks evidence-based dialogue. The focus of collaboration among school and system leaders needs to be more about the effect leaders are having on improving the quality of classroom instruction and enhancing the learning lives of students, and how they are shifting the narrative from test schedules, photocopy budgets, and hiring procedures to a narrative that is about high expectations, growth in relation to inputs, and what impact means. At the heart of this mindframe is the understanding that "success lies in the critical nature of collaboration and the strength of believing that together, administrators, faculty, and students can accomplish great things" (Donohoo, Hattie, & Eells, 2018, p. 44).

The Visible Learning® factors that support this mindframe include collective efficacy, mastery learning, and setting appropriately challenging goals.

Collective Efficacy

Collective efficacy has been the topic of much discussion since it topped Hattie's list of influences from Visible Learning with an effect size of 1.39. The relationship between collective teacher efficacy and student achievement has been well established, dating back to Bandura's (1993) research, which is now almost 30 years old. Consistent findings have been reported in more recent studies as well (Goddard, Goddard, Kim, & Miller, 2015; Ramos, Silva, Pontes, Fernandez, & Nina, 2014; Sandoval, Challoo, & Kupczynski, 2011).

Collective teacher efficacy refers to "the perceptions of teachers in a school that the faculty as a whole can execute the courses of action necessary to have positive effects on students" (Goddard, 2001, p. 467). Collective teacher efficacy is a more powerful predictor of student achievement than socioeconomic status, prior achievement, parental involvement, and home environment. Hattie and Zierer (2018) noted that "clearly, this screams for leadership in the school to develop an organizational climate, create school norms about collaboration, and create the time and direction to enable all teachers in the school to share in this sense of confidence and have high expectations to make the difference" (p. 26). Collective teacher efficacy is fostered through collaboration focused on instructional improvement (Goddard et al., 2015). It is also developed when teachers are mindful regarding evidence about the impact of their teaching (Donohoo et al., 2018). Both of these ideas are embedded in this mindframe: "I collaborate with my peers and my teachers about my conceptions of progress and my impact."

Collective efficacy is also a significant concept related to *principal* effectiveness. *Collective leadership efficacy* refers to principals' shared beliefs about their collective capability to improve student outcomes within and across schools in a district. It is important from a leadership perspective because a growing body of literature demonstrates that "the higher the perceived collective efficacy, the higher the groups' motivational investments in their undertakings, the stronger their staying power in the face of impediments and setbacks, and the greater their performance accomplishments" (Bandura, 2000, p. 78). School improvement initiatives are unlikely to be adopted unless building administrators believe they have the knowledge and skills to execute them well and the ability to provide adequate support to teachers when needed. Furthermore, a firmly established sense of efficacy results in leadership practices that positively influence teachers' motivations.

Collective leadership efficacy refers to principals' shared beliefs about their collective capability to improve student outcomes within and across schools in a district.

When examining the effects of collective leadership efficacy on leadership practices, Leithwood and Jantzi (2008) found effects of collective leader efficacy on school conditions such as (a) minimizing disruptions to instructional time, (b) involving teachers in school decisions, (c) providing feedback to teachers about their instructional practices, and (d) providing adequate time for professional learning. The researchers also found a significant relationship between collective leadership efficacy and students' annual achievement scores.

In districts, collective leadership efficacy is very much influenced by district organizational features such as an unambiguous priority on quality instruction, clear purposes, and the quality of initial preparation along with continued access to meaningful professional learning (Leithwood, Strauss, & Anderson, 2007). Principals' sense of efficacy will be undermined if they feel ill-equipped and underprepared to actively oversee the instructional program and participate with their faculty in learning how to execute instructional improvement work. If conversations center around challenges associated with the neighborhoods where schools are situated, low student attendance, demands that are placed on administrators from the district office, lack of resources, and strong teacher unions, it is likely that collective leadership efficacy will be diminished. In districts where school and system leaders work together to find ways to promote collective responsibility and accountability for student achievement, teachers and students benefit greatly.

The narrative in the district should be less about how to lead and more about the impact of leadership. Are teachers realizing an overall effect of a year's growth for all students in each of their classes? What evidence of impact on teachers' collaborations, their instructional practices, and how they think about their work would convince leaders that they are making progress? What is the quality of teachers' professional learning? These questions are related to adaptive leadership challenges for which there are no clear-cut answers, but it is collaboration with colleagues along with a sense of confidence that better equips leaders to tackle such challenges.

Mastery Learning

Research on mastery learning in classrooms demonstrates that its effect size on student achievement is 0.61. Mastery learning is an educational philosophy that entails cycles of feedback aimed at helping learners attain a high level of performance before moving on to the next stage. Just as mastery learning is important for teachers to foster for students' success (a high-probability influence that Laura Link reinforces in Chapter 8), it is an equally powerful high-probability practice for leaders to foster with teachers to promote teachers' success. In fact, mastery experiences are the number-one source of collective efficacy, and they hold a lot of weight when it comes to building confidence and motivating team efforts (Bandura, 1998). If leaders aspire to create schools and districts where mastery learning is an embedded norm within all levels of the system, there must be a strong belief in the power of collaboration over competition and a willingness to let go of certainty and allow one's beliefs and ideas to be challenged by what others think.

In mastery environments, educators assume a "learning stance," while in performance environments, there is a "knowing stance"—"I know all I need to know in order to do my job" (Donohoo & Katz, 2020). In performance environments, an emphasis on appearing correct takes the focus away from learning and continuous improvement. The focus on individual performance goals and individual incentives further reinforces internal competition, so rather than working as a collective, educators work in isolation.

On the other hand, mastery learning entails educators engaging in joint work (Little, 1990) based on positive interdependence. Teams identify a student learning need (or a teacher/principal learning need) and come together to tackle challenges of professional practice by questioning what they already know and do. Progress is monitored based on success criteria, and feedback is frequent, targeted, and informative. Most importantly, leaders help teams in determining evidence of impact and identifying the next stage in their cycle of professional learning.

Appropriately Challenging Goals

When students set appropriately challenging goals in classrooms, it has an effect size of 0.59 (Hattie, 2019). Locke and Latham (1990) noted that when individuals set challenging goals and receive appropriate feedback, it raises their motivation for success and contributes to better performance. An important conclusion from Locke and Latham's extensive research on goal-setting is that achievement is enhanced based on the degree to which students set *challenging* rather than "do your best" goals in relation to the students' current proficiencies. In this sense, this mindframe is closely related to the fifth mindframe: "I strive for challenge rather than merely 'doing my best.'"

We can turn to two meta-analyses that provide insight into the effect size of goal setting as a leadership practice that influences student achievement. Goal setting was a dimension of effective school leadership identified in Marzano, Waters, and McNulty's (2005) meta-analysis. In Robinson, Hohepa, and Lloyd's (2009) meta-analysis investigating school leadership practices that impact student achievement, establishing goals and high expectations was tied for second place (with "ensuring quality teaching"), with an effect size of 0.42.

Robinson et al. (2009) noted that "goal setting—for both teacher and student learning—is part of a cycle of evidence-based assessment, analysis, and determination of next steps" (p. 109), and this is another reason why it is of particular relevance to this mindframe. In the absence of goals, monitoring progress, realizing collective impact, and identifying the next iteration for professional learning become problematic.

Locke and Latham's (1990) research can be of particular relevance when considering how leaders think about their role in helping teachers (and each other) in setting goals for school improvement. From a leadership perspective, it is about the leader's belief in his or her ability to motivate teachers to engage in the challenges of school improvement. However, it is also about the value leaders place on collaborative goal-setting processes.

WHERE CAN I START?

Focus Collaboration on Instructional Improvement

School leaders play a key role in creating nonthreatening, evidence-based, mastery-oriented environments where the focus is on instructional improvement. Leaders participate with teams as they collaboratively work through an improvement cycle. They do so by fostering open communication about the meaning of impact, engaging teachers in analyzing evidence on the learning progress of students, helping teachers identify student learning needs and corresponding teacher learning needs, assisting teams as they learn about and determine which evidence-based strategies to apply, and encouraging staff to evaluate their progress toward achieving quality implementation.

In addition to participating with teams as they collaboratively work through an iterative improvement cycle (like the one described above), school leaders can also provide teachers with the opportunity to observe each other's practices. When teachers see their colleagues meet with success, it helps to build shared conceptions of progress and impact and it helps to build the individual and collective confidence needed to persist in the work of school improvement.

System leaders also play a key role in setting up the district conditions for instructional improvement. Leithwood and Jantzi (2008) found that the strongest district condition related to collective leadership efficacy was "the district's expressed concern for student achievement and the quality of instruction" (p. 515). Therefore, it is important for system leaders to establish systemic, normative expectations regarding the nature of collaboration within and across schools. They do this by modeling it, ensuring school administrators have access to available research and evidence to inform decisions, and engaging with teams of school principals as they learn how to assess their own contributions to school achievement and consider feedback from others in regard to their leadership practice. Leaders can also co-create success criteria that can be used to identify what leading impactful collaboration entails when it is realized in practice. The success criteria could then be used for self-assessment and as observational "look/listen fors" upon which feedback could be both offered and secured in order to determine steps for strengthening teachers' collaborations through purposeful leadership practices.

Help Teams Identify Shared Mastery Goals

Why is goal setting important? As noted earlier, there is a relationship between goals and motivation. As long as the goal is not too far out of reach, challenging goals raise motivation for success (Locke & Latham, 2006). There is also a relationship between collective efficacy and goal selection. It is partly on the basis of efficacy beliefs that teams choose what goal challenges to undertake. The stronger a team's belief in their collective capability, the higher the goals teams set for themselves (Bandura, 1998). The type of goal can relate to either individuals or teams. Individual goals do little to foster interdependence among team members (Gully, Incalcaterra, Joshi, & Beaubein, 2002). However, when goals belong to the team and outcomes include rewards that are shared by team members and contingent on collective performance, it helps to increase felt interdependencies among team members. A second consideration is related to the goal-setting process. It is important to build consensus among students, staff, and diverse stakeholders about school and district goals. Robinson et al. (2009) also noted the importance of leaders creating a discrepancy between current realities and desired futures. This involves regularly reviewing progress toward goals and frequently reminding stakeholders to consider goals when engaging in decision making about future programs and directions.

Not only does greater collective efficacy result in more challenging goals, but also when goals are met, it helps to boost efficacy even further. As a faculty increases their capacity for sustained improvement, they begin to perceive the difficulty of goals differently. What they may have once viewed as a really difficult challenge no longer seems unattainable. Therefore, it is important for leaders to work with staff in setting progressively more challenging *mastery* goals.

The distinction between performance goals and mastery goals is an important one for leaders to understand. Performance goals undermine long-term performance. In fact, Hattie's (2019) research demonstrates that performance goals have a negative impact on student achievement. They encourage students to adopt surface strategies because the goal is focused on the outcome rather than on the process of learning.

In contrast, mastery goals lead students to use more effective learning strategies and encourage help-seeking behavior. They are also a source of intrinsic motivation. When teams of teachers adopt a mastery orientation toward goal setting, it has the same effect as it does for students. It encourages risk taking, learning from mistakes, and making the necessary adjustments when current approaches are not working.

Progressively more challenging mastery goals would aim to ensure that students are able to transfer their learning to new and novel situations. Rather than focusing on increasing the percentage of students who are *at* or *above* a standard on an annual test, mastery goals focus teachers' efforts on how to help students gain deep, conceptual understandings and how to build students' ability to be assessment-capable learners. When mastery (as opposed to performance) is the goal, it focuses attention on the process of learning and increases learners' (both teachers *and* students) investments in learning. When leaders help teachers set mastery goals, the goals help to encourage teams of educators in figuring out the right balance of surface, deep, and transfer learning; making decisions about how and when to engage students in certain tasks; designing clear learning intentions and success criteria; and gaining deeper understanding of how to frame feedback appropriate to students' instructional level. Mastery goals help teams analyze what needs to be done in order to succeed, which helps to focus teachers' collaborations on instructional improvement. Finally, the research demonstrates that when mastery goals are met, performance goals take care of themselves (Seijts & Latham, 2005).

CHECKLIST

School leaders

☐ believe in the power of the collective;

☐ focus collaboration on instructional improvement;

☐ help teams come to consensus on goals for school and system improvement;

☐ provide feedback to teams about their goals, improvement strategies, progress, and impact;

☐ help teams to set progressively more challenging mastery goals;

☐ assess their own contributions to school improvement; and

☐ take into account feedback about their leadership practice.

EXERCISES

1. Bring together a grade-level team and engage the members in discussion about their students' strengths and most pressing needs. What are one or two evidence-based strategies for addressing the needs identified? How might the team learn more about these strategies?

2. Engage staff in a discussion about the difference between achievement and progress. Ask teams to identify students who fall into the following categories:

    - High achievers - Low progress
    - High achievers - High progress
    - Low achievers - Low progress
    - Low achievers - High progress

      Discuss implications and brainstorm next steps.

3. Ask a colleague to come in to observe you while you engage a teacher team in a goal-setting process. Use the feedback from your colleague and make the necessary adjustments before engaging additional teams in developing mastery goals.

"I AM A CHANGE AGENT AND BELIEVE ALL TEACHERS/ STUDENTS CAN IMPROVE"

Michael Fullan

In 2003, my colleagues and I turned our attention to how to bring about "whole-system" education improvement. We had been studying and writing about the issue for some two decades. I had published my first book on the topic in 1982, *The Meaning of Education Change*. In the fall of 2003, Dalton McGuinty was elected the premier of Ontario—the largest province in Canada. Premier McGuinty had run on a platform of improving public education, which had been stagnant since 1998 when the province had established an arms-length assessment agency, the Education Quality and Accountability Office (EQAO). The EQAO assessed literacy and numeracy at Grades 3 and 6, and again at Grades 9 (math) and 10 (English). Literacy was stuck at 54 percent, and high school graduation rates were holding steady at 68 percent. McGuinty appointed me as his Special Advisor in Education.

We deliberately avoided the grand entrance of establishing a task force and developing a vision, thereby delaying action. Instead, we asked what the more successful districts were doing (change hint: leading practitioners are almost always ahead of research). For example, York Region District School Board (YRDSB), a rapidly growing district with 140 schools just north of Toronto, had been steadily improving its literacy and numeracy scores year after year. We derived some of the key lessons from the York Region success, and added and refined the list (see the eight factors listed below) as a plan of action. You could call this "ready, fire, aim"—not to downplay "ready," as we were building on success.

In October 2003, one week after the election, we met and decided on a plan, expressed on one page. We would have three goals:

1. Increase literacy, numeracy, and high school graduation by twenty or more points.

2. Reduce the gap for students who are underserved (e.g., race, poverty, English as a Second Language [ESL], special education).

3. Increase public confidence in the public education system.

We also decided to establish a new unit in the Ministry of Education that we called the Literacy Numeracy Secretariat (LNS), staffed by over 100 consultants—some from within the Ministry, and many of whom were leading practitioners in the districts that we "seconded" on a rolling basis for three-year terms. Our basic strategy was to invest in *capacity building linked to results*. As leaders, we were change agents who committed to collaboration and getting results—mindframes discussed in Chapters 3 and 4. Capacity building in our case consisted of the pedagogical and change skills of individuals and groups at the school and district levels that would improve learning and its outcomes. We have written more extensively about the Ontario strategy (Fullan & Rincon-Gallardo, 2016), but the core of the strategy consists of the following eight factors:

1. A small number of ambitious goals

2. Leadership at all levels

3. High standards and expectations

4. Investment in leadership and capacity building related to instruction

5. Mobilization of data and effective practices as a strategy for improvement

6. Intervention in a nonpunitive manner

7. Support for conditions/reduction of distractions

8. Transparency, relentlessness, and increasing challenges.

By and large, we were successful across a public system that consisted of 5,000 schools in seventy-two districts, involving over 100,000 educators and two million students. Literacy performance increased steadily from 54 percent to 74 percent over the ten-year period; secondary school graduation increased from 68 percent to 84 percent over that same decade. We also know that it is possible to reduce the gap in focused areas: we all but eliminated the gap between ESL and non-ESL students. In a substrategy called Ontario Focused Intervention Program, we identified over 800 elementary schools that were underperforming. With capacity-building support, that number was reduced to 65 schools. There are still gaps, and we address the question of inequity below, but there is no question that we believed improvement was possible, and we enabled many students to be successful. And we did this with deliberate strategies.

WHAT IS THIS CHAPTER ABOUT?

The vignette above illustrates the success of whole-system reform in Ontario (2003–2013), which was due in large part to one of the most powerful of the Visible Learning® factors: collective efficacy. In the rest of this chapter I will explore the mindframe "I am a change agent and believe all teachers/students can improve," and its implications for deep, lasting, and large-scale system reform. In so doing I will extend Visible Learning factors to apply to whole organizations (schools, districts, states).

WHICH FACTORS FROM THE VISIBLE LEARNING® RESEARCH SUPPORT THIS MINDFRAME?

The 10 Mindframes are clustered into three categories:

Impact

Change and Challenge

Learning Focus

Two of the 10 Mindframe factors are central to our work: subfactor 4 (within "Change and Challenge"), namely, "I am a change agent and believe all teachers/students can improve" (Hattie & Zierer, 2018, p. xv); and subfactor 3 (within "Impact"), "I collaborate with my peers and my teachers about my conceptions of progress and my impact." Stated in terms of the 270+ Visible Learning® influences, three factors stand out: collaborative learning, collective efficacy, and school leadership. Crucially, we will up the ante and ask how the mindframes and Visible Learning influences can apply to not only individual classrooms and schools, but also whole education systems consisting of, in the case of Ontario, seventy-two districts, 4,900 schools, and over two million students. If you believe that all students can improve and that focused collaboration is essential to get there, where do you start when it comes to whole systems?

Collaborative Learning

As we saw in the vignette, effective strategies partnered with willing systems do make a substantial difference in the success of students. But let's examine more closely the concept of collaboration. In a pioneering study of school culture over forty years ago, Dan Lortie (1975) was among the first to clarify that the existing culture of schools favors stagnation. He found that the work of teachers was characterized by three mutually reinforcing traits: presentism (what do I do today); conservatism (solving small-scale, immediate problems); and individualism (working in isolation). In 1990, Judith Warren Little captured this syndrome of stability in the phrase "the persistence of privacy." While there seemed to be agreement that such a culture should change, we can conclude that many of the efforts in the four decades since Lortie's study can be characterized as superficial attempts at teachers working together.

The good news is that there has been a shift in the past five years or so toward more precise and powerful collaboration—a change in depth that is entirely compatible with the 10 Mindframes. At the core of this more powerful collaboration is the reframing of "professional capital"—human, social, and decisional capital (Hargreaves & Fullan, 2012). There is nothing automatically good about collaboration. People can collaborate to do the wrong things, or to do nothing. After several decades of superficial debate about collaboration, researchers and practitioners are finally sorting out the good from the weak or ineffective forms of collaboration. Hargreaves (collaborative professionalism), Fullan (connected autonomy), Datnow and Park (the purpose of collaboration), and Donohoo (collective efficacy) have all recently pinpointed what kinds of collaboration have a positive impact. Essentially, the findings are that a combination of several factors—high expectations, transparency of practice and results, relative nonjudgmentalism, greater precision (not prescription) of practice, high-yield strategies, assessment and use of data, learning from each other, and participatory leadership that supports all of these practices— combine to generate success in student learning.

Collective Efficacy

This brings us back to the heart of this chapter. Hattie's finding that collective efficacy yields an impact size on student learning of 1.39 dramatically reinforces my argument. This finding blew the lid off the coefficient ensemble, with most findings well below 1.0. The Visible Learning constellation of collective efficacy consisted of four interrelated factors: high expectations; evidence of impact; high-yield strategies; and leaders who participate in frequent, specific collaboration with teachers. In short, it is the combination of certain factors that makes the difference.

In many ways, the findings about collective efficacy confirm on a wider scale why Ontario was successful. It has become clear that regular schooling is no longer fit for purpose. There is a great deal of data to show that students are increasingly bored or worse as they go up the grade levels, and that being a literate high school or university graduate does not mean that you will become good at life or even survive in increasingly complex times. For the past five years, we have moved into the new arena of deep learning as the possible answer (Fullan, Quinn, & McEachen, 2018; Quinn, McEachen, Fullan, Gardner, & Drummy, 2020). The learning focus and outcomes of deep learning are the 6Cs: character, citizenship, collaboration, communication, creativity, and critical thinking. The immediate learning supports are the four design elements: partnerships, pedagogies, learning environment, and leveraging digital. And the combination of all of these factors must be supported by the leadership conditions in the school, district, and policy environments.

The stakes are much greater: worsening world conditions, galloping inequity, lower trust and cohesion, and a much more complex agenda. Can we still believe that all students can learn? The answer may be more optimistic than is the case under the comparatively straightforward agenda of the basic skills tackled by Ontario. Students are rising to the occasion because the conditions and solutions appeal to their deeper nature. We are discovering two related deeper truths: one is that most students are attracted to doing something worthwhile. We have labeled this "Engage the world Change the world." The 6Cs, enabling pedagogy, and collective pursuit enabled by teachers as partners are generating massive active participation in learning. Second, and even more profound, we are finding that all students benefit from deep learning, but it is especially beneficial for students who are alienated or otherwise disconnected to regular schooling. We are systematically testing this hypothesis; it would represent a significant finding because we may be able to conclude that it is possible to reach virtually all students, even those historically most alienated from schooling.

Leadership

Finally, I would say that the concept of leadership must be extracted from Visible Learning research as well as the wider literature. It is not explicitly in the mindframes, although adopting these mindframes is an implicit part of being a change agent as a leader. Some elaboration on the critical role of leadership in the new era is needed.

The answer to the challenge—all students can learn—depends on leadership, and a particular kind of leadership at that. New leadership, to use a concept that was the title of my most recent book, must be *nuanced* (Fullan, 2019). Nuanced leaders see details below the surface, while also seeing the big picture. They participate as learners; they can be experts on some things and apprentices on others. They know that every time they change jobs, they become automatically deskilled (because they know that there are things they are bound not to know about the new context). They know because of

NEW LEADERSHIP

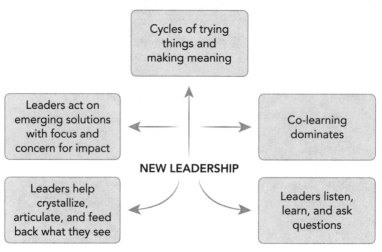

Source: Fullan (2019).

Figure 4.1

complexity that plans must be jointly determined and mutually adapted. They know that accountability is achieved internal to the culture through transparency and developmental support. They tackle deeper problems and build courage through action. They go outside to get better inside. Figure 4.1 captures some of the cycle.

In addition to being a lead learner, the effective leader helps develop other leaders as they go. Our expression for this is that the modern leader develops other leaders for six or more years to the point where they become dispensable. At that point, they know when they depart that the organization can carry on without them. Their legacy is continued and deepened leadership in the organization for the future.

WHERE CAN I START?

Aside from attaching oneself to good mentors, the best place for a leader to start is to heed the advice to "go slow to go fast." In other words, start by building relationships with those you work with in order to build the change agenda together. The checklist that follows provides some guidelines for building the conditions for having a disproportionate impact on learning within an organization (see Fullan, 2019).

CHECKLIST

☐ Have curiosity about what is possible, openness to other people, sensitivity to context, and a loyalty to a better future.

☐ See below the surface, enabling participants to detect patterns and their consequences for the system.

☐ Connect people to their own and each other's humanity.

☐ Teach, rather than lead.

☐ Change people's emotions, not just their minds.

☐ Have an instinct for orchestration.

☐ Foster sinews of success.

☐ Be humble in the face of challenges, determined for the group to be successful, and proud to celebrate success.

☐ Build accountability into the culture of the organization.

☐ Be courageously and relentlessly committed to changing the system for the betterment of humanity.

Leaders can also begin the discussion about leading productive collaboration by engaging in the exercises that follow.

EXERCISES

Exercise A

Form groups of three.

Each person records one example that they experienced where collaboration was effective.

Record one where it was not productive.

Share ideas.

On a flip chart, draw a line vertically down the middle.

On the left side, list the common characteristics of ineffective collaboration.

On the right side, list the characteristics of effective collaboration.

(Continued)

(Continued)

Think of your own situation: Identify steps you might take to combine mindframes 3 (collaboration for impact), and 4 (being a change agent to improve learning for all).

Exercise B

Rate yourself on each of the three competency domains from Lead Learner Competencies (Fullan, Quinn, & Adam, 2016). On a scale of 1–5, how often do you engage in the twelve habits listed (1 = low; 5 = high).

A. Model Learning
   i) Participate as a learner.
   ii) Lead capacity building.
   iii) Make learning a priority.
   iv) Foster leadership in others.

B. Shape Culture
   i) Build relational trust.
   ii) Establish structures and processes for collaborative work.
   iii) Engage others in complex problems.
   iv) Resource strategically.

C. Maximize Learning
   i) Focus on precision in pedagogy.
   ii) Establish a small number of goals.
   iii) Create a clear strategy for achieving goals.
   iv) Monitor impact on learning.

Conclusion

In short, believing that all kids can learn and being a leading change agent are one and the same. Leadership that focuses on impact must shape and navigate the pathways of jointly determined deep change in practice. Leaders who participate as learners are essential for forging unity of purpose and its implementation.

"I STRIVE FOR CHALLENGE RATHER THAN MERELY 'DOING MY BEST'"

Zaretta Hammond

The middle school is located in a working-class neighborhood in San Francisco. Fifty percent of its students are eligible for free and reduced lunch, and the population is a rich mix of racial, ethnic, and linguistic diversity. Joe Truss, the principal, has worked hard with staff to create a positive school culture and climate. It's reflected in the school's motto: *"We work hard to create a positive school climate where students are recognized for their growth."*

As the school leader, Mr. Truss and his leadership team worked hard to help teachers improve the adult culture and student climate. By every measure, the social-emotional tenor of the school had improved. Yet, when the staff sat down to review its quarterly achievement data a few years into the process, it was clear that improvement in relationships and belonging wasn't translating into improved instruction or increased student learning. He recalls a particular spring staff meeting where they gathered to look at data. Many teachers expressed concern and confusion. They thought for sure academic scores would change. Many shrugged their shoulders in defeat, pointing out they were "doing their best."

However, Mr. Truss wasn't satisfied with the status quo when it came to student learning. He took on the challenge of helping staff build on their climate success and going to the next level with a focus on improving student learning through academic conversation. He thought it was the perfect vehicle for improving instruction by giving students more ownership and opportunity for meaning making. But he soon realized that the same teachers who worked diligently to improve the climate for the children and their families held low expectations and deficit thinking around their students' readiness as learners to carry academic dialogue and discussion. This approach was going to require more self-directed student learning and more capacity building to help all students be active participants, especially those learning English. This reality stretched many teachers beyond their comfort zone. Teachers had gotten used to compliant student behavior—being quiet, talking only to answer questions, and going along with lecture as the primary mode of sharing content. He remembered teachers expressing skepticism about students being able to handle the levels of independent learning necessary for effective academic conversations to flow in ways that went beyond the superficial to deepen understanding.

"We were talking specifically about supporting students to use academic conversations in the classroom to build their skills to do project-based learning," he recalled. "I heard teachers saying things like, 'Well, I don't feel comfortable letting them talk at length,' or, 'I don't feel comfortable when I'm not holding the whole class together. What's going to happen to my classroom management if I turn over control to them?'" Others agreed. "I can't trust that they're going to be on task," another said. How does the leader challenge the staff to go beyond "doing their best" to move to their "growing edge," which can feel scary? He challenged them to get smarter together, using a multipronged approach that included collaborative inquiry and professional development around student and teacher capacity building rather than a singular focus on the technical solution of one-off strategies.

WHAT IS THIS CHAPTER ABOUT?

The vignette illustrates this chapter's main message: improvement requires challenge—challenging our mental models about what students can do, challenging our teacher beliefs about pedagogy, and challenging deficit thinking that holds us back from becoming warm demanders of students' cognitive development. School leaders recognize that we won't achieve equitable outcomes simply by "doing our best." The mindframe in this chapter highlights an important point about leadership: *change can be challenging for adults*, and it is the main job of the school leader to help people navigate the challenges of change rather than retreat into the status quo of "doing our best," especially when trying to advance instructional equity that builds students' learning muscles.

When you finish reading this chapter, you should be able to take this message as a basis for explaining

- how the significant Visible Learning® factors of instructional leadership, collective efficacy, and monitoring teaching impact on learning work together to synergistically move the needle on equity;

- why "doing your best" can be an expression of deficit thinking rather than lack of effort, and what a leader must do to challenge limiting beliefs about the learning potential or motivation of diverse students; and

- what we need to understand about "change management for equity" that leverages challenge in positive ways in adult learning communities.

WHICH FACTORS FROM THE VISIBLE LEARNING® RESEARCH SUPPORT THIS MINDFRAME?

Teacher Estimates of Achievement

The factor of teacher estimates of achievement is foundational to educational equity. If teachers don't believe in certain groups of students' capacity for growth, based on race, culture, linguistic capacity, or socioeconomic status, then their efforts to accelerate learning through powerful teaching will be limited. What complicates this Visible Learning® influence is the history of racial segregation and colonization in the United States and other countries. In the past, to justify systems of racial segregation and colonization, many institutions, including schools, perpetuated a set of deficit narratives of racial difference. Despite slogans like "all kids can learn," many of those deficit narratives are still with us.

The one heard most often in school settings is what microaggression expert Dr. Derald Sue calls "the ascription of intelligence" (Sue et al., 2007). This narrative says that certain racial groups have more intellectual capacity than others. In her book *SchoolTalk: Rethinking What We Say About and to Students Every Day,* Mica Pollock, Professor of Education Studies and Director of the Center for Research on Educational Equity, Assessment, and Teaching Excellence (CREATE) at the University of California, San Diego, points out that these negative narratives about which groups are smart and which are not as smart play out in schools in cloaked and coded ways that she calls "smart talk" (Pollock, 2017). Too often, we readily accept these unexamined beliefs about the limited capability of diverse, historically marginalized students to self-motivate, actively engage, or productively take on rigorous learning to explain chronic achievement gaps. These deficit beliefs are mostly unconscious and often go unexamined.

School leaders have the challenge of surfacing and dispelling these narratives that drive teacher estimates of student achievement. That means articulating what success looks like so that teachers don't mistake cultural differences in learning for intellectual deficits. An equity-focused school leader understands that just telling teachers to have "high expectations" doesn't get rid of deficit thinking, nor does implicit bias training alone. Instead, he or she is skilled in helping teachers trace these deficit narratives in their instructional decision making and then leverage professional learning processes to support the construction of new narratives about student capacity by proving them wrong through collaborative inquiry.

Collective Efficacy

Once teachers have high estimates of achievement for all students, school leaders have to leverage collective efficacy to ensure that all students are making significant progress toward high levels of learning. Collective efficacy is the perception of teachers in a school that they possess the necessary skills and that the efforts of the faculty as a whole will have a positive effect on student learning. From a school leadership perspective, it means helping staff develop a shared belief that their collective skill and knowledge in teaching can push student outcomes to higher levels, especially for those who have been historically disadvantaged.

Too frequently, educators get caught up in the "*pobrecito* syndrome." *Pobrecito* roughly translates from Spanish into "poor baby," and the "syndrome" is how Dr. Pedro Noguera, author of the book *The Trouble With Black Boys . . . and Other Reflections on Race, Equity, and the Future of Public Education* (2008), describes well-meaning people who don't expect much of students who are poor or from a historically marginalized racial group. The thought goes, "Poor baby, of course he's going to underachieve, he's disadvantaged!" As a result, a teacher may feel that he or she is doing his or her best for a student with perceived limited intellectual capacity. Collectively, teachers may feel they cannot accelerate student learning to get more than a year's growth in a year's time when students are far behind grade level. Instead, they opt for "protecting" the students by lowering the bar rather than building their adult capacity to help students carry more of the cognitive load during instruction.

Because of this misguided desire to protect the self-esteem of poor or so-called "minority" students, we often accept these narratives and the resulting "poor baby" stance that lowers expectations and dials down rigor. Many teachers have been told that a quiet, compliant classroom is the pinnacle of success, while the research is telling us that for students to be academically successful, they must be active, cognitively independent learners who can accelerate their own learning. School leaders with an equity focus help teachers understand the elements of a successful learner's habits of mind and skills. The school leader doesn't let teachers mistake cultural differences for intellectual deficits. Instead, he or she is able to articulate a rich description that values and leverages students' funds of knowledge and ways of learning that lead to academic success.

In addition, the school leader helps articulate what successful teaching looks like that develops this type of student. He or she shows the symbiotic relationship between teaching and learning, focusing on instructional decision making and pedagogical content knowledge rather than "one-size-fits-all" strategies.

Providing Formative Evaluation

When we think about instructional leaders who are monitoring teacher performance, we often picture them doing surprise walkthroughs and conducting classroom observations in the back of the room with clipboard in hand, evaluating teacher performance frequently. Part of instructional leadership is shaping the path toward success—supporting and evaluating teaching through regular classroom visits and provision for formative and summative feedback to teachers. School leaders who provide formative evaluation are focused on getting everyone in the school working together to monitor teaching impact on learning. According to leadership researchers such as Michael Fullan (2015), the research suggests that there is greater impact when the school leader helps the faculty get focused around a small set of core pedagogies, and then creates a culture of reflective practice aimed at helping teachers get better at coaching student "learning to learn" processes rather than launch new initiatives to raise test scores. The learning leader focuses on encouraging "safe-to-fail," small-scale experiments that allow emerging possibilities to become observable—teachers can see small student changes that can snowball into big learning gains. These small experiments are not just random stabs in the dark or focused on strategy implementation. Instead, they are anchored in sound pedagogy and spotlight student learning moves.

The school leader who strives for challenge is also leading adult learning by paying attention, along with the staff, to the cause and effect of teachers' new instructional moves on changes in students' awareness of their ability to manipulate their moves to improve performance. This means the school leader creates the conditions for several different types of feedback loops for both teachers and students (e.g., learning conferences as part of assessment for learning structures, student-led conferences to increase student agency and awareness as learners). Some schools have used Japanese-style lesson study or "Looking at Student Work" protocols as part of their formative feedback loops.

Others have focused on Jim Knight's (2007) instructional coaching method to help teachers become aware of instructional decision making that changes students' awareness of their learning. Monitoring our impact on student learning and seeing changes we didn't believe were possible can be the catalyst for reshaping our mental models about student capacity and motivation based on deficit narratives we didn't realize we'd internalized. In addition, the school leader is creating a social-emotional container for adults to manage their own emotional responses to challenge and being stretched into their zone of proximal development.

WHERE CAN I START?

Being a school leader who strives for challenge and creates the conditions for others to do the same requires that they first build their own emotional intelligence and social-emotional capacity to support other adults through change, especially when addressing issues of deficit thinking, low expectations, and underdeveloped instructional practice that decelerates student learning.

Assess Current Reality So You Can Understand What's Producing the Outcomes

School leaders can benefit from taking time to assess the current status of the mental models influencing teacher decision making. Too often we jump to a solution without really understanding the problem. When we strive for challenge, we begin by understanding the nature of the challenge. To do that, you have to first understand the system that produces the results you are currently seeing play out in classrooms. Take two to four weeks to get a sense of the "systemness" in your building. Systemness is a term coined by Michael Fullan (2015) and it means the way different parts of a school's policies and practices come together and create an outcome or result that wouldn't happen by any of the individual components acting by themselves.

Model Using Errors as Information for Improving

Often teachers need to see what it looks like to use different types of data, including failed attempts or prototypes, to improve. Using the principles of improvement science, let them see you engage in rapid cycles of inquiry to try high-influence strategies and fail fast to quickly improve some aspect of your school leadership or school process. This helps teachers see failing not as a bad mark against them, but as information to be used to get better. It also requires making time to do a postmortem on failed prototypes to understand what went right as well as what went wrong and why.

Leverage Social Neuroscience to Make Challenge Feel Fun and Doable

Managing our emotions is an important part of embracing challenge. School leaders must understand the neuroscience behind change and challenge. Incorporate activities that get teachers' brains to reduce the stress hormone cortisol, and instead focus on activities that release dopamine. Dopamine is connected to our perseverance in the face of doing hard things. It makes us lean into a challenge and helps reduce the anxiety and stress related to it.

CHECKLIST

Consider the following the next time you engage in school improvement planning:

☐ Ensure teachers are able to surface the mental models that influence their expectations by discussing the dominant narratives that you were exposed to as an educator.

☐ Work toward shared agreement with your teachers about which teaching moves lead to student learning success.

☐ Create structures and reallocate time to support teachers working together to improve their practice.

☐ Create a variety of feedback loops, including tools like video and low-inference transcripts that provide timely formative data to help teachers iterate on their instructional decision making.

☐ Pay attention to your own cultural competence and emotional intelligence as you manage the social-emotional side of change in your adult learning community, especially when addressing historical inequities.

EXERCISES

1. Build your stamina and fluency for talking about issues of deficit thinking disguised as merely "doing our best." Start with *scripting*. For two weeks, practice active listening across your school and try to identify the three or four most common statements about "those

(Continued)

(Continued)

kids" or "those families," or other deficit-oriented comments that come up in various settings. Then, taking one statement at a time, write a script for how you would respond to such statements in the future.

2. Model using low-inference transcripts and video as forms of feedback in low-stakes ways to get teachers and coaches comfortable using them to gather data in their classrooms.

3. Create a thirty-day or sixty-day challenge across the school to encourage small, high-leverage changes among your faculty until these changes become new habits or old habits are broken. Notice what gets in the way of making the changes.

"I GIVE AND HELP STUDENTS/ TEACHERS UNDERSTAND FEEDBACK AND I INTERPRET AND ACT ON FEEDBACK GIVEN TO ME"

Peter M. DeWitt

VIGNETTE

Your principal makes the announcement that they are looking for student engagement when they complete this week's walkthroughs. Although you do not know what the principal does with the walkthrough information, you are ready for this one because student engagement is your passion. As a teacher, you regularly activate experiences where students are engaged in dialogue around learning. You consistently circle the classroom listening in and offering feedback where necessary. A walkthrough focusing on student engagement is a welcomed opportunity. However, your principal enters the classroom, looks around at all the students moving about talking with each other, and makes one of two statements: (1) Your classroom management needs some work, or (2) I will come back when you're teaching. Not exactly the feedback you were expecting.

So, what happened? We often have common language without common understanding. Feedback and student engagement are two areas where not having a common language and a common understanding can create an untrusting school climate.

WHAT IS THIS CHAPTER ABOUT?

This chapter is about how school leaders need to not just provide feedback to teachers and students, but also create opportunities to have dialogue focused on feedback where all parties in that dialogue learn from one another. Too often school leaders approach dialogue as if it is something that they need to give, but leaders need to receive and learn from feedback as well.

Feedback has been a popular topic in schools over the past decade. Research shows that feedback has the potential to accelerate student achievement (0.66 effect size according to Hattie, 2019) and is something adults in schools are craving. The issue is that it is often one-sided and presents itself as a criticism focused on something the giver doesn't see in learning or the classroom, rather than something the teacher or student cares about.

The opening vignette portrays a scenario that often plays out in schools between a school leader and a teacher. Although they were talking the same language when discussing student engagement, they did not have a common understanding of what student engagement *means*. Let's build a common understanding now as we focus on feedback.

WHICH FACTORS FROM THE VISIBLE LEARNING® RESEARCH SUPPORT THIS MINDFRAME?

Teacher–Student Relationships

In Hattie's meta-analysis of 270+ influences on learning, teacher–student relationships have an effect size of 0.48. School leaders and teachers need to understand that relationships are an important place to begin when thinking about how to provide students with effective feedback. Students will be much more receptive to feedback from a teacher with whom they have a relationship, and the same can be said for the relationship between a school leader and a teacher. Relationships are at the core of how teachers, students, and school leaders operate in school. When they are strong, they can take the ebb and flow of learning, where sometimes feedback is easy to take and other times it's a little more difficult to hear.

Teacher Credibility

Teacher credibility has a 1.09 effect size and means how credible students believe their teachers are when it comes to the learning process. There is a simple reason why this influence on learning is integral to the feedback process. When students see their teacher as a credible source, and when teachers see their school leaders as a credible source, and vice versa, the feedback process is stronger. Stone and Heen (2014) researched feedback triggers, which prevent a receiver from fully accepting the feedback they receive. One feedback trigger is the relationship trigger, which is set off when the receiver does not believe in the credibility of the person providing the feedback.

School Leadership

In over 600 studies, including seventeen meta-analyses, school leadership has an effect size of 0.37. Although that is below the hinge point of 0.40, which equates to a year's worth of growth for a year's input, it is important to highlight school leadership as an important influence in relation to feedback, because one moderator in the school leadership research is that of instructional leadership. Instructional leadership is one of the most researched forms of school leadership over the past fifty years, and it has an average effect size that falls just above the 0.40 hinge point.

Instructional leaders understand that they must talk about learning at faculty meetings, engage in walkthroughs or learning walks where teachers and the leader have a common understanding of the walkthrough focus, and engage in observations that focus on instructional strategies that will have a positive impact on student engagement. School leaders who engage in authentic dialogue around learning, and who develop a common language and common understanding around those strategies included under the instructional leadership umbrella, such as walkthroughs, discussion of instructional strategies, and a focus on student engagement, become more credible when offering effective feedback.

Credibility is highly important because one of the critical practices of instructional leadership is the provision of formative and summative feedback to teachers. Thus, instructional leaders need to understand and effectively apply all aspects of the feedback process, which includes the gradual release of responsibility from the feedback giver being in total control, to gradually letting go of some of that control and turning it over to the learner. However, it is important to understand that regardless of a person's role in the feedback process (i.e., receiver, giver of feedback, school leader, teacher, or student), all parties should approach feedback as something they can give to one another. After all, feedback is a two-way street.

The Four Feedback Levels

Figure 6.1 portrays the four different types of instructional feedback: self, task, process, and self-regulation.

THE FOUR DIFFERENT TYPES OF INSTRUCTIONAL FEEDBACK

Feedback	Proficiency needed	Gradual release of responsibility	Role of feedback giver
Self	Unrelated to specifics about the task	N/A	Complementor
Task	New material	I do	Teacher
Process	Some degree of proficiency	We do	Coach
Self-Regulation	High degree of proficiency	You do	Mentor

Figure 6.1

Hattie and Zierer (2018) state, "Task level [feedback] happens when the feedback lets students know when the answer is correct or incorrect and whether they meet the criteria for success" (p. 94). When considering this level of feedback at the adult level, task-level feedback happens between a school leader and teacher when the teacher lacks experience with the strategy being used. Perhaps it is a new instructional strategy for them, like reciprocal teaching or the jigsaw method. In this case the school leader will provide feedback focusing on whether the teacher used the instructional strategy correctly or not. They provide feedback on how to improve the implementation of the instructional strategy.

Process-level feedback is present when students and teachers engage in dialogue around the "strategies the students applied in the learning process or whether the student can detect errors in their work" (Hattie & Zierer, 2018, p. 94). At the adult level, process-level feedback may take place when a teacher has a deeper level of understanding of the strategy. Using the example of reciprocal teaching or the jigsaw method, the school leader would watch the teacher teach a lesson using one of those instructional strategies, and talk with students about what they are learning and how they are grasping the concept. For example, when specifically looking at reciprocal teaching, the school leader will talk to students to see if they understand their role in the process, and ask questions to get an understanding of how the strategy is helping them learn the material being taught. Make no mistake; although the school leader may be the one with experience in the strategy being used to teach a learning intention, both the teacher and the school leader engaging in co-teaching should be open to learning from one another.

Self-regulation feedback takes place when students "provide reasons for having completed a task correctly or incorrectly" or "when they can explain their success" (Hattie & Zierer, 2018, p. 95). In our adult examples between a teacher and a school leader, self-regulation feedback happens when the teacher does their own self-reflection of a goal they set with their school leader, is able to detect ways to improve their practice, and is aware of which students are improving and which may need more or a different teaching strategy. The aim of feedback by the school leader is to evaluate these claims to help the teacher evaluate their impact, and here is where gradual release of responsibility to the teacher is most optimal. This often happens after teachers and school leaders grow through task-level and process-level feedback around a specific goal, but it also may happen based on the fact that the teacher has a deep level of understanding on a particular goal already. Using the instructional strategy or student engagement examples, the teacher uses evidence to understand their impact on student learning, and shares that with their school leader as part of a continuing conversation around a goal.

One specific example of how self-regulatory feedback may happen is when a school leader and teacher meet to discuss a goal the teacher wants to pursue during the year. Perhaps that goal focuses on increasing student engagement through cooperative learning. During the goal-achieving process, the teacher and school leader use Google Keep to house all of the evidence they keep in pursuit of the goal. When the school leader does a learning walk or walkthrough, they take specific pictures of students that capture the engagement in learning and upload those pictures into the Google Keep folder. When the teacher is alone with students, and the students are working cooperatively without the direct aid of the teacher, the teacher may take some photos and upload them into the same folder along with evidence to show how well the lesson went. When the school leader and teacher can schedule time together, the teacher takes the school leader through the evidence they uploaded.

When a clear understanding of learning intentions and success criteria is not present, feedback is often at the "self" level—unrelated to specifics about the task. This means that the feedback provided is actually more praise than anything directly related to learning, and, although it feels good to get a compliment, it doesn't often help guide learning to a deeper level. This happens for a number of reasons. One reason was used in the opening vignette of this chapter. The school leader and the teacher lack a common language and a common understanding. Another reason is that it happens when a school leader lacks credibility. If school leaders do not engage in dialogue around learning, they will most likely not be able to provide effective feedback to teachers, which means they are highly at risk of remaining in the self level of feedback.

It is important to understand that feedback should be directly related to the level of proficiency of the student or teacher of feedback. For example, if it's new material for the student or teacher in their learning journey, then they need to be provided with task-level feedback because they do not have deep experiences in the content being learned.

As you can read in Figure 6.1, the role of the feedback giver is that of the typical teacher role where they understand the content and therefore help the learner to see where they went wrong in their answer. The gradual release of responsibility becomes a situation of "I do," where I will help break this learning down to its most basic element to keep the learning somewhat simple.

When teachers and students move from surface to deep learning, and then from deep to transfer learning, the role of feedback changes and becomes more complex, and the gradual release of responsibility shifts from the teacher being the fountain of knowledge to the student taking more of a role in their own learning. Process and self-regulation feedback take place when the learner becomes more confident in their own learning. Through this process, teachers are experiencing growth because they are learning how to scaffold their feedback at the same time that they are learning how to let go of some of the control they have in the classroom in order to transfer some of that locus of control to students.

Three Questions That Lead Our Way

Hattie and Timperley (2007) suggest that feedback is "conceptualized as information provided by an agent (e.g., teacher, peer, book, parent, self, experience) regarding aspects of one's performance or understanding" (p. 81). The important aspect to that definition is that the receiver of feedback should be involved in dialogue to build understanding, and not be on the receiving end of a feedback sheet, which is often how feedback is provided.

Too often teachers and school leaders jump up to grab feedback because it is a piece of low-hanging fruit in the research, but they do not always research how to provide the best and most effective feedback, which means their feedback is at risk of creating more issues than it may help solve. The most important place to begin when discussing feedback are the three questions of Visible Learning®:

Where am I going?

How am I going?

Where to next?

When teachers and school leaders have those three questions in mind as they design surface, deep, and transfer learning opportunities, and when they help their students and teachers understand the importance of each one of those questions, the feedback process will become much easier and much more impactful. Why? Feedback is best when it focuses on a learning intention and success criteria. Focusing feedback around a learning intention and success criteria is the first major step to ensuring feedback has the maximum impact. This was a much-needed step in the vignette that led us into this chapter. If the principal and teacher in our example had established the learning intention and success criteria together, the results of the walkthroughs would have been much more positive. Although the process is complex and involves a great deal of prepping and practice, including students in the construction of learning intentions and success criteria can be the most impactful way to maximize student learning.

The three questions of Visible Learning provide a framework for school leaders, teachers, and students to maintain a clear path through the learning process. In order to gain the best understanding of how to put this into practice, school leaders need to be responsive to the needs of teachers and make discussions about feedback one of the topics of faculty meetings, professional learning communities, walkthroughs, and teacher observations.

Observations and Walkthroughs

As we know, feedback is important for everyone who is involved in the learning process. Many times school leaders talk to teachers about the feedback those teachers need to provide to students, but the quality feedback school leaders provide to teachers about their own practice is equally as important. Unfortunately, that feedback often misses the mark. In the opening vignette, the school leader is looking for student engagement in the classroom, which the teacher facilitates flawlessly, but because the teacher and the leader do not share a common understanding of what student engagement is, the feedback provided was misdirected and most likely created more of a negative experience than a positive one.

These days, it is very popular for school leaders to do walkthroughs. Walkthroughs are meant to allow school leaders, or a leadership team (e.g., consisting of both administrators and teacher leaders), to walk into classrooms and get a sense of the learning that students are experiencing. A key component of walkthroughs is feedback, which usually means that school leaders leave feedback sheets or checklists for teachers to get a sense of their performance level in specific situations. Unfortunately, when school leaders leave a feedback sheet for teachers, that feedback may not have anything to do with the focus for the students and teachers, or—worse—the school leader completely missed the way the teacher and students were learning the content. Perhaps the teacher and students were engaged in a classroom discussion technique that the school leader mistook for a random conversation not focused on learning at all. Why? Perhaps that school leader was looking for more of a lecture design where the students were sitting and listening as the teacher was talking.

In the formal observation process, school leaders are responsible for providing feedback about the teacher's performance during a lesson. Leaders are supposed to meet with teachers in a pre-engagement session focusing on the intentions of the lesson, and then they observe the teacher for 45 minutes to one hour, and then within a certain number of days they meet up with the teacher for a post-observation meeting to discuss what the leader saw in the observation. Unfortunately, too many times school leaders cite their busy schedules or the lack of a requirement by their central office as reasons for not meeting with teachers prior to the formal lesson. Therefore, they do not have a full understanding of the learning intention and success criteria for the lesson they are observing. Those school leaders look for the learning intention and success criteria up on the whiteboard or interactive Smartboard when they are sitting in the back of the room watching the teacher, and when they do not see it, they mark down that the teacher did not have it.

What if they approached the situation a bit differently? What if, instead of sitting in the back of the classroom, they sat next to students and asked them what they were learning or what the learning intention of the lesson is, to see how the student responds to the question? If a school leader actually talks with the students, they can determine what the learners understand and allow the students to provide better and more effective feedback.

This process opens up the feedback loop to include leaders, teachers, and students and provides an opportunity for all of these stakeholders in the school community to have a stronger focus on feedback.

WHERE CAN I START?

Walkthroughs and formal observations are some of the most important responsibilities of leaders and some of the most effective vehicles for feedback. Done correctly, these activities can provide a great deal of learning for the teacher and the leader, and ultimately the learner. Done wrong, they can destroy a school climate and help promote compliance rather than any quality learning.

School leaders can help set up an important structure in the feedback process by providing a space for teachers and school leaders to engage in dialogue around feedback where they develop a common language and common understanding. Additionally, school leaders need to have a deep understanding of how to provide, accept, and act on the feedback as well. Walkthroughs, faculty meetings, and professional learning communities are important places to not just offer feedback but to learn about it, too.

CHECKLIST

☐ Develop a common language and common understanding of feedback.

☐ Involve students in the creation of learning intentions and success criteria to deepen their learning.

☐ Understand the four levels of feedback (self, task, process, and self-regulation) identified by Hattie.

☐ Understand that feedback is about engaging in dialogue around learning; it is not a one-sided conversation.

☐ Ensure that the receivers of feedback see the givers of feedback as credible sources.

EXERCISES

Try approaching observations by doing the following:

Preconference—Ensure the school leader and the teacher share a common language and common understanding about what will be observed. Discuss what academic vocabulary and understanding the students should be able to articulate about their learning during the lesson. Define the learning intention and success criteria of the lesson that will be observed. Teachers do not have to have it hanging up in the room for students to understand it. Define what it is before the walkthrough or observation.

Walkthrough/Observation—Talk with students. Do they understand the learning intention and success criteria? Are they engaged in dialogue with their peers, and providing correct and authentic feedback to their peers during the lesson? Are students able to use the academic vocabulary the teacher has taught them?

Postobservation—Provide feedback to the teacher around the learning intention and success criteria. How many students were actively engaged? Were any of the students confused by what they were supposed to be learning? Does the teacher have any feedback for the leader when it comes to the walkthrough or observation process?

EXERCISE

Try approaching feedback conversations by doing the following:

Preconference—Ensure the school leader and the teacher share a common language and common understanding about what will be observed. Discuss what academic vocabulary and understanding the students should be able to articulate about their learning during the lesson. Why might reciprocal teaching or the jigsaw method be the best strategy to engage students in their learning goal?

Walkthrough/Observation—Talk with students. Do they understand the learning intention and success criteria? Are they engaged in dialogue with their peers, and providing correct and authentic feedback to their peers during the lesson? Are students able to use the academic vocabulary the teacher has taught them? This will help guide more authentic feedback from the leader to the teacher.

Postobservation—Provide feedback to the teacher around the learning intention and success criteria. How many students were actively engaged? Were any of the students confused by what they were supposed to be learning? Does the teacher have any feedback for the leader when it comes to the walkthrough or observation process?

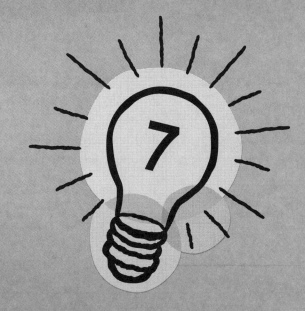

"I ENGAGE AS MUCH IN DIALOGUE AS IN MONOLOGUE"

Douglas Fisher, Nancy Frey,
and Dominique Smith

VIGNETTE

Dominique, a school administrator, joins the ninth- and tenth-grade teachers from Health Sciences High as they start their team meeting. The meeting starts with teacher leader Kim Elliott reminding the group of their meeting norms, which they developed collaboratively at the start of the year. She then turns their attention to the assignment analysis that they agreed to use the previous week. Ms. Elliot begins, "Last week we agreed to review a writing task that students would complete. We wanted to spend some time on the complexity of the assignment to ensure that students are expected to perform at an appropriate level of mastery. Then when we look at the impact, we'll be sure that it's at the right level of complexity."

There are eleven teachers in the room, and they take turns providing analysis of the assignment. Dominique listens. At one point, a teacher asks, "What will we do if students don't pass? What interventions do we need to have in place?" The codeveloped grading policy at this school focuses on mastery rather than compliance and allows for students to retake assessments to demonstrate success. One of the mottos of the school is that "it is never too late to learn." But that doesn't mean that all students learn the content the first time, despite good planning and support. The team begins to focus on the systems that they want to put in place to help students who do not succeed.

Dominique enters the conversation saying, "Can I ask a couple of questions? A few weeks ago we talked about students using the assessments we give them as practice knowing that they can redo them later. I was reading a study about practice testing and thought maybe we could develop some practice assessments so that students would have a better sense of their performance and then wouldn't use the 'real' assessment for practice. Maybe then we wouldn't have as many students needing additional support. Thoughts?"

The conversation is lively. One teacher asks for examples of practice tests, saying, "We don't just give tests, but I wonder if this would work for projects and essays as well." A peer responds, "I've been struggling with this. In math, they really seem to use the assessment as practice. I think that they learn a lot over the year, but their scores on the first assessment are lower and then we have to engage in a reteaching and support. I think this could be a really good move."

The conversation continues, and Ms. Elliot guides the team to a decision. They will each use a practice assessment in the next week, teach students how to analyze the results using an item analysis tool, and then identify appropriate study skills. They will then give another practice version or "real" version, depending on where they are in their unit of study, and determine the impact. They decide on a common format to start, which requires that students categorize their responses into one of four areas:

Easy items I got wrong	Easy items I got right
• These are things that need practice	• These are skills I have mastered
Complex items I got wrong	Complex items I got right
• These are things I still need to learn (and I can use peers or the teacher for help)	• These are things that I can teach others

WHAT IS THIS CHAPTER ABOUT?

This case study highlights the role of the school leader in listening and engaging in dialogue with teachers. We think of dialogue as a give-and-take of ideas that lasts at least sixty seconds (and probably longer). To realize the potential of this mindframe, leaders must learn the skills of dialogue and practice those skills regularly.

Imagine, instead, if Dominique had come into the meeting and announced his new learning and implied (or worse, demanded) that teachers implement practice testing. There are times when leaders need to be clear on their expectations for teachers, similar to the way that teachers must be clear about their expectations for students. For example, at the school Dominique leads, there is an expectation that parents, students, and colleagues receive responses within one workday. There is also an expectation that learning intentions and success criteria are posted in every classroom for every lesson.

Having acknowledged that sometimes the school leader must make his or her expectations clear, the daily operation of the school requires that school leaders engage in more dialogue than monologue. A monologue occurs when the leader tells people what to think or do. During a dialogue, leaders listen and respond, share thinking, ask questions, and work to reach consensus. Robert Garmston and Bruce Wellman (1999) describe four ways of talking:

- *Conversation* consists of convivial, casual, friendly talk about personal and social matters; it's usually not directed or facilitated.

- *Discussion* is talk that has a purpose—often to make a decision. Discussion may seem unstructured at first as people brainstorm ideas and explore possibilities, but it becomes more structured as people choose sides. It may, in fact, begin to resemble debate.

- *Debate* is an extreme form of discussion in which the format dictates that people take sides and advocate for that side, rebutting points from the other side. Debates are usually structured and formal; they leave no room for compromise or building on others' ideas.

- *Dialogue* is more structured than conversation, but less structured than discussion or debate. Dialogue engages people in building their understanding of an issue without the pressure to make decisions or be "right." People inquire into ideas, rather than advocate for their own or others' ideas. Doing so builds trust, which is critical to creating a climate in which teachers feel comfortable working (Tschannen-Moran, 2014).

WHICH FACTORS FROM THE VISIBLE LEARNING® RESEARCH SUPPORT THIS MINDFRAME?

We consolidate our understanding when we interact with others. As we engage in dialogue with others, we have an opportunity to extend our thinking and clarify our own understanding. Through interactions with others, our ideas can be challenged and we may come to a new understanding. It is this give-and-take that ensures that ideas are interrogated and understood. In terms of an organization, people need to feel involved and valued if they are going to commit. When school leaders engage in excessive monologues, teachers and other school staff are less likely to feel a sense of ownership in the organization and may not commit as deeply to the mission. When teachers feel involved, through dialogue about important issues, they tend to dedicate themselves to the organization and work to accomplish its goals. Several influences from the Visible Learning® database are helpful in understanding why dialogue is important for school leaders, including school climate, collective efficacy, and microteaching.

School Climate

School climate has a positive impact on student learning with an effect size of 0.43 (Hattie, 2019). Simply said, climate is the feel of the organization and is often noticeable to people as they enter the building. School climate has been the focus of research for over 100 years (e.g., Perry, 1908) and has a reasonable influence on a variety of factors such as student achievement, effective violence prevention, and teacher retention (Thapa, Cohen, Guffy, & Higgins-D'Alessandro, 2013). As Cohen, McCabe, Michelli, and Pickeral (2009) noted, "School climate is based on patterns of people's experiences of school life and reflects norms, goals, values, interpersonal relationships, teaching and learning practices, and organizational structures" (p. 180).

Every school has a climate, whether it be positive or negative. The climate is fragile and changes as part of the evolving history of the school. Leaders must engage colleagues in dialogue, in part to nurture the climate of the organization. As Cavanaugh (2016) notes in her book *Contagious Culture*, we must individually and collectively understand that how we "show up" each day is contagious. A school's climate is influenced by the attitude we bring to our work. In other words, our actions and words send powerful messages to our colleagues that can either build their individual and collective efficacy or harm it. As leaders, we must create safe places—physically, emotionally, and intellectually—for students and teachers to learn.

School leaders should regularly and systematically monitor the climate of their school and use the results of monitoring to develop action plans to create, strengthen, and/or maintain the culture of their school. There are a number of tools useful in this endeavor, but we are partial to those developed by the Quaglia Institute (www.quaglia.org), as they have instruments for students, staff, and families to share their perspectives about the climate of the organization. But even more important than the data are the inferences groups make about the data and the corrective actions they take. It is the dialogue we have, with our colleagues and our students, about what the data mean that can shine a light on what needs to be done to maximize the power that the climate has to impact student learning.

Collective Efficacy

The power of the group and the value of dialogue as part of a team's interactions are demonstrated in the effect size of collective teacher efficacy, which stands at

1.39 (Hattie, 2019). As Jenni Donohoo discussed in Chapter 3, collective teacher efficacy is a complex concept but a valuable one to cultivate, given its influence on learning. To our thinking, there are two major parts to this idea. First, impact is realized when a group of educators has systems for determining what students need to learn; has concrete plans to ensure that learning; and measures their impact, making adjustments when students do not learn as expected. Second, this group of educators believes that their students can learn and that the group has the power (skills, knowledge, beliefs) to ensure that students learn. As Bandura (2000) noted, "Unless people believe that they can produce desired effects and forestall undesired ones by their actions, they have little incentive to act" (p. 75). Mastery experiences are among the most powerful ways to build collective efficacy (Bandura, 1986). When teachers practice together actions and strategies to promote student learning, they can determine where their strengths and weaknesses lay. This is one of the most powerful sources of efficacy information (Tschannen-Moran, Woolfolk Hoy, & Hoy, 1998). When groups of educators experience success and accomplishment, they begin to attribute those successes to their actions rather than outside forces.

To facilitate mastery experiences, we have developed a collective efficacy learning cycle (see Figure 7.1). Our model starts with a common challenge. The operative word here is *common*, which means that the group agrees upon it. And that means that they had an opportunity to talk about it. School leaders should not simply analyze data in their offices and announce goals to teachers. Instead, groups need to grapple with the data and identify goals that will challenge them. There is evidence that groups with a strong sense of collective efficacy set higher goals for themselves (Goddard, Hoy, & Woolfolk Hoy, 2004).

Through dialogue with teachers, school leaders can help teams identify their common challenge and what they would like to see as an outcome. From there, teams set forth on a learning journey. Highly efficacious teams understand there is still much to learn, but they remain open to a variety of learning opportunities. Sometimes, they read books, articles, or websites. Other times, they attend workshops or seminars. The format is not important. What is important is the realization that there is learning that the team can do together.

As they learn, team members engage in what we call *safe practice*. They get to try on ideas and test them out. They get to fail and learn from their mistakes. At this stage, leaders are listening and engaging in dialogue with teachers and not simply observing them and giving critical feedback. Teachers are given the opportunity to try out new approaches without the anxiety of having others watch.

Naturally, this will lead to *opening up practice*. Again, dialogue is critical. Groups with strong collective efficacy do not simply replicate strategies from their peers,

A CYCLE FOR PROMOTING COLLECTIVE EFFICACY THROUGH PROFESSIONAL LEARNING

Source: Fisher, Smith, and Frey (2020).

Figure 7.1

but rather deepen their understanding about the nuances of the approaches their peers use. This stage also invites vicarious experiences in which teachers learn from watching each other, noting the impact that the instruction has on student learning. Vicarious experiences are an additional way that collective efficacy can be built (Bandura, 1986). Peer learning during this period of safe practice builds the belief systems of the team that they can accomplish their goals.

When practice becomes more public, the effect of modeling is mobilized. Modeling and social persuasion are also valuable in creating and maintaining collective efficacy, even if they are not as powerful as mastery experiences (Bandura, 1986).

And, perhaps most importantly, highly efficacious groups monitor, measure, and modify. They track successes and note their impact. This information feeds the group as they continue their efforts. The group begins to see their efforts, rather than outside factors, as the source of impact. That is not to say that everything a group with high collective efficacy tries works the first time. The difference is that they *monitor, measure, and modify* their efforts to achieve the common challenge. They attribute the success they experience to their efforts and set new goals the next time around the cycle.

School leaders have to understand this cycle of building, maintaining, and reinforcing collective efficacy. The leader's role is to collaborate and engage in substantive dialogue with teachers.

Microteaching

A third way that student learning can be impacted through dialogue between adults is microteaching. With an effect size of 0.88 (Hattie, 2019), microteaching is worthy of attention. Not too many years ago, it would have required a rather Herculean effort to video-capture teaching and learning. Many people did not have portable video equipment with high-quality sound capabilities. But now we all do. Our phones and tablets are excellent devices for capturing learning environments. But simply video-recording classrooms is not going to result in the impact that we need.

It is the dialogue about the footage that has the potential to create change. In far too many cases, observations focus on what the teacher was doing rather than on what students were learning. In a traditional observation without video footage, the observer tells the teacher what he or she saw. This invites differences in opinion and recall bias. The observer, often with detailed written notes, tries to prove his or her point, while the person being observed becomes defensive. Microteaching cuts through that. Videos are used to encourage the teacher to notice the moves he or she is making as well as the impact those moves have on student learning.

During a microteaching conversation, the focus is on short segments of the video, dissecting teacher moves and students' responses to those moves. To start, we encourage leaders to invite teachers to select the segment for discussion. We recognize that many educators are wary of being recorded as they fear that the "evidence" could be used against them. Microteaching is about growth and impact and therefore trust needs to be established for this to work. We encourage leaders (including teacher leaders) to consult with teachers in advance and clearly outline the appropriate and inappropriate uses of the recordings. For example, in some places the digital files are deleted after the interaction. In other places, the observer uses the teacher's technology to record so that the file is never in the observer's hands. In addition, we encourage people to start with volunteers who are interested in improving their students' learning and allow for the practice to spread over time. We believe that the day is coming in which microteaching, using clips of video to discuss the learning experience with a colleague, will be commonplace (Shaw, 2017).

Importantly, conversations about the videos as part of microteaching should not focus on a laundry list of all of the things that the teacher did wrong. We have developed a list of sample questions that can be used during a microteaching conversation (Fisher, Frey, Almarode, Flories, & Nagel, 2020):

- What did you want your students to know and be able to do?

- What connections have you made?

- What did you see or hear that confirms your previous thinking?

- What did you see or hear that conflicts with your previous thinking?

- Which moments did you find to be particularly effective?

- Which moments did you think did not go as well as you had hoped?

- What was different in comparing those moments?

- What would you change in order to accomplish your stated goal?

- What do you want to be sure to do again? (p. 98)

As Manna (2015) noted, principals are magnifiers and multipliers of effective teaching. Actually, we think that school leaders have the *potential* to be magnifiers and multipliers of effective teaching, but it only happens when they engage in more dialogue and less monologue. Unfortunately, they might also engage in actions that harm the climate of the school and reduce the collective efficacy of their teachers. As Hattie (2019) notes, the impact of principals is just below average with an effect size of 0.37. We need to increase our effectiveness and impact by making sure that high-probability practices spread across the school and take root.

WHERE CAN I START?

We don't mean to be flip, but stop talking so much. Listen more. You might even record your next conversation with a group of educators and play it back to see how often you are dominating the conversation versus how much time you are engaged in a dialogue. If you are not yet practicing this mindframe, we suggest that you take a note from the cognitive coaching playbook. Some key dialogue skills include the following (www.thinkingcollaborative.com):

- Pausing—take time to listen fully to others before responding.

- Paraphrasing—rephrase what you think you heard and ensure that you understand the perspective of others.

- Posing questions—ask questions to encourage people to share their thinking and to ensure that you understand the thinking of others.

- Putting ideas on the table—when you understand others, you can add information to the conversation. Try to focus the conversation on the idea rather than the positional power you have.

- Providing data—give groups information to work with and allow them to draw inferences from the data.

- Paying attention to self and others—notice your emotional state and non-verbal language and ensure that it aligns with your message (everyone else in the group is already noticing).

- Presuming positive intentions—assume that members of the group want the best for students and are willing to work toward that outcome.

CHECKLIST

The following items will help you engage in more dialogue than monologue:

☐ Assess the climate of your school

☐ Talk with others about the data and formulate a plan

☐ Introduce the collective efficacy cycle and invite groups to identify their common challenge

☐ Monitor the amount of talking versus listening that you do

☐ Find volunteers to engage with you in microteaching

EXERCISES

1. Record, with teachers' permission, the next team meeting. Notice your moves. Did you pause? Paraphrase? Which of the moves described above dominate your style? What do the data say to you about the value you place on dialogue?

2. Plan a professional learning session in which teachers experience an "early win," meaning that they accomplish something meaningful for which they can attribute their efforts to the success of the group. From there, introduce the power of collective efficacy and work to build the experiences of your teams.

3. Take a risk and teach a lesson. Video that lesson and engage in microteaching with teachers on your campus. Show them that you are vulnerable and that you listen to their feedback.

"I EXPLICITLY INFORM TEACHERS/ STUDENTS WHAT SUCCESSFUL IMPACT LOOKS LIKE FROM THE OUTSET"

Laura Link

During Aboite Elementary School's first faculty meeting of the academic year, Principal Miller celebrates her teachers and administrative team for their 34 percent average student growth last year, which represents 104 more students reaching mastery (a grade of A or B) on instructional learning units. She commends the significant summative assessment improvement in Grades 3–5, in which 20 percent more students reached mastery on end-of-year cumulative exams. Principal Miller points to their focused collaboration and shared expectations for meeting student targets and expresses confidence in all teachers' readiness to meet this year's student growth goals as well.

Principal Miller also thanks teachers for their input in creating this year's teacher expectations and year-end goals for students. She notes both can be found in the Teacher Handbook and in the "welcome back" letter sent to teachers over the summer. Principal Miller reminds teachers of their agreed-upon expectations for meeting the success criteria, which means they will work to

1. organize instruction into learning units directly tied to standards,

2. create two parallel formative assessments for each learning unit,

3. provide students with multiple corrective activities using different modes of engagement for each learning unit,

4. provide students with multiple rewarding and challenging activities for each learning unit, and

5. document student progress at the individual and classroom level.

Principal Miller also reminds teachers that they will review and reference the documented progress data against year-end student growth goals during their formative evaluation conferences together. Based on teacher input, Principal Miller shares her newly created formative evaluation conference schedule that includes the specific dates and times teachers will meet with her, or a member of her administrative team, to discuss their Tables of Specifications (success criteria) aligned to their planned parallel formative assessments for their first learning unit. She communicates that this formative process, like last year, will enable her and her administrative team to provide and seek feedback from teachers based on their agreed-upon success criteria for instruction and formative assessments, and that the feedback will be regular and ongoing throughout the year. She emphasizes how she looks forward to observing teachers' first instruction as well as their corrective instruction, which takes place after teachers analyze their students' formative assessment results. Principal Miller tells teachers that she firmly commits to doing her part, including holding the expectations steady and providing them regular goal-referenced support so that together, they can once again meet students' growth goals at the end of year.

WHAT IS THIS CHAPTER ABOUT?

As illustrated in this case study, clarity is the key to outstanding performance. To be effective, teachers should know at any given time what is the most important work they can do to contribute to students' success and how well they're doing at it. However, too often, school leaders fail to prioritize clarity and provide poor communication, ill-defined goals, and inadequate feedback and evaluative processes (Tuytens & Devos, 2016; Wahlstrom & Louis, 2008). Such ambiguity causes teachers to reach inaccurate conclusions, make faulty decisions, or spin their wheels in nonproductive ways. With clarity, teachers *and* students can be efficient and engaged. Clarity helps them feel more confident, capable, and connected to school priorities and problem solving (Smith, 2018; Welch & Hodge, 2017). To be sure, clarity is not easy to achieve. But the clearer school leaders can be in defining goals and expectations, providing specific support toward those goals, and using agreed-upon metrics for success, the more teachers and students will perform to their fullest potential (Fullan, 2009; Sanders, 2014).

WHICH FACTORS FROM THE VISIBLE LEARNING® RESEARCH SUPPORT THIS MINDFRAME?

Ultimately, school leaders are responsible for establishing the organizational supports that build growth-enhancing cultures for teachers and students. In fact, there's little debate that school leaders play a critical role in both individual and systemic improvement efforts (Fullan, 2009, 2014; Leithwood, Louis, Anderson, & Wahlstrom, 2004; Link, 2019; Papay & Kraft, 2016; Saphier, 2017). Yet, simply being in the role of school leader isn't enough. Leadership that impacts teacher and student success first requires clarity of teacher goals and teacher expectations towards meeting those goals.

Teacher Clarity

Just as teachers must make learning intentions and success criteria visible for their students, school leaders must make learning intentions and success criteria visible for *teachers* at the start and throughout the school year to ensure a school-wide focus that optimally impacts student learning. Clear goal intentions has an effect size of 0.51 (Hattie, 2019). Teachers need to know what's expected of them so they can plan effectively and structure their instruction and assessments so students can reach the intended year-end performance goals. This requires clear and repeated statements of expectations in multiple ways over time. But simply having goals and expectations alone will not automatically result in higher teacher performance and higher student achievement. School leaders must put in place the organizational supports, such as mastery learning and formative evaluation, to create classroom environments conducive to learning (Papay & Kraft, 2016).

When goals and expectations are not clearly in place, ambiguity arises. Ambiguity about student learning goals and teacher expectations means not having to work to satisfy them. It also creates an opportunity for biases and assumptions to influence how information is interpreted (Smith, 2018; Suftka & George, 2000). Ambiguity tempts school leaders and teachers to make idiosyncratic decisions that lack consistency from teacher to teacher. It also prompts school leaders and teachers to be reactive: instead of addressing the most important issues, they address those attracting attention at the moment. Ambiguity prevents schools and districts from operating with focus, alignment, and engagement—all necessary enablers for student learning (Guskey & Link, 2019).

As a result, when school leaders work within the mindframe of "I explicitly inform teachers/students what successful impact looks like from the outset," clarity is prioritized, allowing teacher and student performance to thrive.

Mastery Learning

Developed by Benjamin Bloom (1968), mastery learning is a practical strategy school leaders and teachers can use to create a classroom structure for learning, so more students learn at high levels. As an influence on student achievement, mastery learning achieves an effect size of 0.61. The basic idea of mastery learning is that when students are given sufficient time and appropriate instruction, they can learn well and master the course concepts and skills.

With mastery learning, clear specification of students' learning goals is of critical importance so teachers can use those goals to offer students regular and specific feedback on their learning progress. The clear goals also help teachers and school leaders identify the instructional steps necessary to reach those goals. For example, mastery learning emphasizes that all students are afforded *diagnostic* feedback on their learning; that is, the information students receive should identify precisely what they were expected to learn, what they have learned well to that point, and what they need to learn better (Guskey, 2010). Students who do not achieve mastery are provided *prescriptive* feedback that identifies the specific concepts and skills they need to spend more time on through corrective activities. By first establishing mutual expectations as to how teachers will meet such student feedback and corrective goals, school leaders can provide teachers with more precise feedback on their implementation efforts during routine classroom observations. Additionally, school leaders can secure from teachers their own self-assessment against the established goals, revealing teachers' misconceptions or confusion that can lead to improved performance for both teachers and students.

A recent evaluation showed that teachers involved in year-long mastery learning pilots saw a 25 percent increase in the number of students reaching mastery (a grade of A or B) on classroom assessments across all grade levels and subjects (Link, 2018). Mastery learning provides all students with differentiated instruction (Tomlinson, 2006) and more favorable learning conditions where they can meet the outlined goals and expectations (Guskey, 2010).

Formative Evaluation

Michael Scriven (1967) was the first to identify a distinction between formative evaluation and summative evaluation when describing the two major functions of program evaluation. To Scriven, formative evaluation is intended to foster development and learning improvement *during* a programmatic process, whereas summative evaluation is used at the *end* of the process to assess results. Benjamin Bloom (1968, 1971) incorporated this notion into the mastery learning classroom instructional process through the use of formative and summative assessments. To Bloom, formative assessments are instruments used to provide feedback to both students *and* teachers. Depending on function, any assessment can be used to make a formative evaluation (during the lesson) or summative evaluation (at the end of a lesson) (Hattie & Zierer, 2018). Therefore, the evaluative function and utility of assessments comes from how they are used. As an influence on student achievement, formative evaluation has a 0.34 effect size in the Visible Learning® research.

When teachers use assessments to make formative evaluations, the results are used to help teachers gain valuable insights from students in order to help teachers better understand their impact and adjust their instruction based on results. Formative evaluation provides important information to teachers on what is happening in their classroom so that they can ascertain "How am I doing?" in achieving the learning intentions they have set for the students, such that they can decide "Where to next?" for students.

As a form of feedback, formative evaluation has a specific aim: focus on the goals of the learning process and determine whether the learners have reached the goals (Hattie & Zierer, 2018). It prompts both teachers and school leaders to determine how students are progressing toward their current learning unit goals *and* overall year-end goals.

The first step toward effectively implementing formative evaluation includes school leaders and teachers clearly defining students' year-end goals, designing actions toward achieving those goals, and offering goal-related information about those actions together (Wiggins, 2012). Thus, improving learning depends on teachers' ability to adjust instruction based on an ongoing measurement of student progress against concrete learning unit goals and overall year-end goals. If utilized effectively, formative evaluations can reinforce the specified grade-level or subject area criterion for success and help teachers more precisely articulate progress toward that success to both students and their parents throughout the year.

School leaders are the main evaluators of teachers' performance (Isoré, 2009), so when school leaders regularly focus on teachers' progress toward their own and students' year-end learning goals, the impact on teacher growth and student

Formative evaluation provides important information to teachers on what is happening in their classroom so that they can ascertain "How am I doing?" in achieving the learning intentions they have set for the students, such that they can decide "Where to next?" for students.

performance is substantial (Marzano, 2012; Mielke & Frontier, 2012). To offer effective formative evaluation to teachers, school leaders supply more than the typical comments about what they observed during a teaching period. Instead of only informing teachers that their lesson is on track for the day's goal, school leaders should use formative evaluation to continually inform teachers whether they're on track to achieve the desired level of student performance by the end of the school year.

To accomplish this, school leaders and teachers first co-construct the formative evaluation success criteria together and regularly use them to inform teacher practice throughout the year. Creating specific success criteria allows both teachers and school leaders to get clear on what's expected for well-implemented practice and to have a tangible tool to evaluate performance quality against the specific year-end goals.

WHERE CAN I START?

One of the most important steps in cultivating this mindframe is clearly defining the criteria for success at the start of the school year. This requires knowing in the fall where you want student performance to be in the spring—and teacher performance throughout the year. School leaders must move beyond communicating ambiguous expectations such as asking teachers to "build a positive classroom culture" or "create engaging work" for students, then leaving teachers to figure out the meaning on their own. Instead, at the start of the year, effective school leaders engage teachers in dialogue about learning success and instructional processes. Collaboratively, they create agreed-upon criteria for success from which student *and* teacher progress is measured, feedback is sought and provided, and instructional decisions are made. The success criteria serve as the anchor for shared understanding, actionable feedback for teachers, and a tangible reference toward meeting year-end goals. No more evaluations in which teachers are unclear about how they're performing against the success criteria. And no more lessons in which students are not shown the success criteria at the start or offered feedback on how to improve without referencing them. Commitment to this communication process allows school leaders and teachers to stay focused and see success with greater clarity together.

CHECKLIST

☐ Formulate success criteria with teachers from the start.

☐ Articulate teachers' expectations for meeting the success criteria at the start of the year.

☐ Provide organizational support, such as mastery learning, to give structure to teachers' expectations and make the success criteria visible.

☐ Conduct regular conversations with teachers to ensure they understand and are aligned in using the success criteria.

☐ Observe both teachers' instruction and how they use student assessment results.

☐ Use formative evaluations to regularly inform teachers about their performance toward meeting the success criteria and students' year-end goals.

EXERCISES

1. Self-assess your use of success criteria to measure and inform teacher performance. Discuss your self-assessment with a colleague.

2. Plan your next school year using mastery learning. Discuss your planning and coordinate implementation with teachers.

3. Conduct regular conversations with teachers about their performance toward year-end goals. Compare/contrast with a colleague the information gained versus solely conducting instructional observations of teachers.

> ## "I BUILD RELATIONSHIPS AND TRUST SO THAT LEARNING CAN OCCUR IN A PLACE WHERE IT IS SAFE TO MAKE MISTAKES AND LEARN FROM OTHERS"
>
> Sugata Mitra

Terminal Velocity

"I don't want to do this," I thought.

I mean, it's not that I didn't want to do it, whatever it was, it's just that I had no idea what this long vertical glass tube filled with oil was for and why I was standing in front of it.

It was 2 p.m. on a sleepy Monday afternoon in my physics lab, and Mr. Grover was staring fixedly at me. Well, actually, not at me, but his way of looking was such that everyone thought he was looking fixedly at them. Cool trick, he must have practiced it. Mr. Grover was the principal of my school and had a lot of office work to do to keep things going, but he loved these lab sessions and often came to observe.

Impressed by Mr. Grover, I tried looking fixedly at the glass tube in front of me. It was about as tall as I was and had lines marking centimeters on it. My staring at it did not produce any results.

Mr. Grover strode purposefully toward me. Taking immediate evasive action, I started to read the instructions pasted on the wall behind the tube, squinting with great concentration. It turned out that there was no need for panic, because Mr. Grover simply muttered, "You need glasses, Sugata," as he passed toward the door at the far end of the lab.

The thing is that Mr. Grover encouraged teachers to let us work things out for ourselves. He called it "self-organizing," and we liked it. It's just that he was the principal and we were a bit careful about him.

"Do you know what this thing is for?" I asked Rita, as soon as Mr. Grover passed by. She was very bright and everyone asked her everything.

Well, it took Rita less than three minutes to explain that I had to drop a steel ball into the tube and measure its velocity at the top, middle, and bottom. The ball speeds up as it falls and then it stops speeding up and moves at the same velocity downwards. "It reaches terminal velocity," she said, giggling for no reason.

My best friend, Roy, along with Rita and I then went online and it took a few minutes to figure out that the force of gravity on the ball was exactly balanced by the resistive force of the oil at a certain point and velocity can't change if there is no force.

This was right, as I found out with my glass tube, steel ball, centimeter markings, and a stopwatch. I dropped the ball on the floor twice in the process and said "damn" only once. Everyone laughed. Even Mr. Grover had the hint of a smile on his face. He thought I had done really well. I liked that.

WHAT IS THIS CHAPTER ABOUT?

This chapter is about relationships and trust, and both of those are related to the perception of threat.

Perception of threat is the cause of fear.

Let's construct an imaginary Threat Perception Meter (TPM). Let's say it has a needle that swings from left to right across a semicircular band. The band is colored green toward the left moving on to yellow in the middle and then to red toward the right. The TPM tells you how threatened you feel at any time. For example, out for a walk in the park, if you see a huge dog break out of its leash and start running toward you, the TPM needle will move into red. Or, if you come back from work and smell gas in the kitchen, the needle will move to yellow. On the other hand, if you are in front of the TV with a coffee, the kids are quietly doing their homework, and your partner is out fixing the fence, your TPM needle is in the green.

We think differently, depending on whether our threat perception is green, yellow, or red, and the leaders in our schools have a direct impact on determining that culture of learning.

Fear and Learning

Red

When our threat perception is high, we have difficulty learning anything. Our brains are in the fight-or-flight mode. This is not the best mode to be in for comprehension or analytical thinking.

When teachers are measured by the average scores of their students on tests, when parents insist on these scores as the only measure they care for, both students and teachers perceive threat.

If teachers or learners feel threatened, they will be reactive, and their actions will be based on short-term goals. Sometimes, even governments can be in such modes of thinking, thus spreading their fears through the education system. At such times, school leaders have to stand between the school and short-term goals—an unenviable job.

Surface motivation (–0.14), depression (–0.26), and boredom (–0.47)—all negative influences from the Visible Learning® list of effect sizes—are active when threat perception is high in an educational setting.

Yellow

When our threat perception is low, but not absent, we are careful about what we learn. One part of our brain is occupied with monitoring and managing any emergent threats, while the other part struggles with learning. This is why learners can freeze when a watchful teacher approaches them. This is why the best of teachers cannot answer simple questions in the presence of a critical school leader. In the vignette above, we, the students, were in the yellow condition in spite of a benign and friendly principal. We still had to wait for him to leave before we self-organized.

All performance is threatened by the possibility of failure. Teachers and students are not meant to perform. Students are meant to learn, and teachers are meant to assist with students' learning. A school leader should create the environment where this can happen. One example of this kind of environment is a SOLE: Self-Organized Learning Environment.

> Teachers and students are not meant to perform. Students are meant to learn, and teachers are meant to assist with students' learning.

If you do enable a SOLE, things will happen by themselves. Groups of children, figuring things out by themselves, using the unfettered Internet, will head toward the right kind of learning, correcting errors as they go along. The yellow will change to green.

Green

An absence of threat is when minds are free to wander or engage with ideas. This is the highest level of human consciousness to which a learning environment can aspire. Very young children, such as those in elementary (also called "primary") schools, often feel this safety, or absence of threat and fear. They respond instantly with a barrage of questions. They become free, noisy, collaborative, and engaged. Unfortunately, as the years go by and there is an emphasis on knowing rather than learning, we find that students ask fewer and fewer questions. School leaders can prevent this loss with relationships and trust.

I have seen the benefits of leaders who allow and encourage children to self-organize to pursue learning, detailed extensively in my 2019 book, *The School in the Cloud*. In twenty years of research, we found over and over again that children can self-organize and learn in evolving groups, all by themselves, when appropriate resources are provided. It can be intimidating for teachers and school leaders to let go of control and allow kids in the green zone to pursue learning on their own. The fear is that without enough guidance, students won't learn. And yet the research found consistently that students in self-organizing environments arrived at the right answer time and time again.

Let's take a deeper look at how school leaders can help cultivate this type of environment.

WHICH FACTORS FROM THE VISIBLE LEARNING® RESEARCH SUPPORT THIS MINDFRAME?

The learning influences that support this mindframe are the following:

1. Questioning: This is the magic wand of pedagogy—and of leadership, for that matter. Entire processes can be driven by questions alone. Socrates showed us this 2,500 years ago!

2. Strong classroom cohesion: The teacher and students are working together toward positive learning goals.

3. Collective teacher efficacy: Teachers believe that they can affect their students' learning.

Self-organization needs collaboration, and collaboration needs trust. This is nature's way of getting things done. An atmosphere of trust is entirely different from an atmosphere of accountability. "Without a level of trust, teachers, like most people, will close ranks, put up barriers and retreat to old and tried methods behind a closed classroom door," as Raymond Smith so aptly put it while he was reviewing this chapter.

A school leader can affect all of these. This is the most important and the most interesting thing a school leader can do.

Questioning

Down the ages, from Socrates to Freud, we have seen the power of questions as tools for shaping minds, but still we hesitate to use them. School leaders are often expected to have all the answers, and yet there is great power in modeling your willingness to question as a way to inspire teachers and students to ask bigger and better questions as well.

The best school leaders—ones who encourage environments where kids have intrinsic motivation to learn—start by asking, "Is there a better way to learn? How can we give students more ownership over their learning?"

Questioning is vital at the classroom level, too. The teachers' ability to raise the right questions at the right levels of student ability is the key to getting a SOLE to work well. This is the new learning leadership in our connected age. Make the questions too easy and you make the process meaningless. Make them too hard and the collective loses confidence. Learning stutters and stops. At such times, encouragement is crucial for the trust to continue.

Strong Classroom Cohesion

Classroom cohesion is an often-overlooked influence in the Visible Learning® research, and yet it has great potential to accelerate learning with an effect size of 0.53. Classroom cohesion is characterized by trust and mutual respect (between leaders, teachers, and students), and it focuses on supporting all students in their learning. Trust: There is an assumption any human being can make about another, and that is that the other person is really good at something. If you make that assumption about every teacher and student in your school, you should find out what those key strengths are. Trust is built on strengths and not weaknesses. Unfortunately, in existing systems of assessment, the emphasis is often about weaknesses.

In the story at the beginning of this chapter, the principal had succeeded in building the courage in a group of students to find things out for themselves, even if they did so when he left the room! Yes, students will be wary of a principal no matter what, but the little smile from the principal when they get it right makes up for it all. And he did ignore the times I dropped the steel ball on the floor, so good for him.

Collective Efficacy

Here are two kinds of atmospheres you could create, if you are a school leader:

1. Safe, boring, and predictable. Your school runs like a well-oiled machine. If you create this atmosphere well enough, you are almost not required anymore. Is it your job to make yourself obsolete?

2. Safe, but unpredictable. Your school is not like a machine; it is like a garden. Things happen there that are not always predictable. And those unpredictable things can lead to unexpected results. You are required there all the time, not always able to help, but always there. You are the gardener—you can't tell your plants how to grow, but you can be with them, loving them, listening to them, helping when you can, and most of all, admiring them.

Ironically, scenario 1 above would easily fit the three highly effective learning influences well. In your machine-like, predictable school, teachers would easily believe that they can influence students' learning as much as they have done before, and exactly as much in the future. Students will predict their own and their peers' performance exactly—exactly as they have done in past years and exactly as they will in the future. Teachers will predict their students' performance in subjects and skills, based on what they have observed before and expecting the predictable nature of the school machine to produce the same in the future. You, the school leader, should be a happy camper under these conditions, should you not?

Such schools were the dream schools of the twentieth century. They produced our best minds and our worst monsters.

Scenario 2 will need a lot of thought. You don't make things happen; rather, you plant seeds that let things happen. You encourage the exploration of the unknown. "Is there another way to do this?" you ask. Your school deals with the biggest questions of our times, no matter what the subject or curriculum is. Your school imagines what the future might be like. Now, John Hattie's top three learning influencers become the most exciting and perhaps the most difficult things your students and teachers have ever done.

Can your teachers still collectively believe they can affect their students' learning? Only relationships and trust can nurture and strengthen that belief. And you are there to help the seed germinate.

I have a colleague who is really good at reading Thematic Apperception Test (TAT) scores. It's a gift she has. At the same time, she is quite bad at statistics. If I were to focus on improving her statistical skills, I would never be able to trust her. Instead, I trust her TAT reading skills immensely. She understands that.

An assessment report, for a student or a teacher, should start with "This person is really good at . . ." It should not end with "The areas for improvement are . . ." An apple tree is really good at making apples; would you suggest it could be improved to make bananas as well?

WHERE CAN I START?

The Physical Space

We often underestimate the importance of the physical school environment on building relationships and trust. You can relate to and trust people only when you find them in an environment that fosters such qualities.

Put your students and teachers in a safe, functional, and aesthetically pleasing environment and it will be so much easier for things to fall into place. Fill your school with as much natural light and fresh air as possible. Try alternative flooring options such as wood, soft tiles, carpet, or even Astroturf, as I saw one innovative school leader do in the United Kingdom.

Encourage creativity and collaboration by using walls as writing surfaces. Seats should be easy to move around so that children can create their own groups and decide where they want to sit.

The effect of the physical environment is often overlooked by school planners. Stephen Heppell's work on this is an eye opener (http://heppell.net/home/).

The Method of the Grandmother

Believe it or not, self-organized learning is helped along by admiration! Think about how a grandmother admires her grandchildren (I say "grandmother" in a stereotypical sense; it could be anybody, male or female of any age). She encourages them to go further in their learning through simple statements such as, "My goodness, how did you understand that?" "Show me again how you did that," or "I could never understand that myself." She has genuine affection for her grandchildren, and they know it and thrive on impressing her with their ability.

This simple emphasis on admiration is the role a school leader can play in any school. It's the role Mr. Grover played for me, and it spurred me to greater understanding of velocity. As you observe classrooms and interact with students, ask them about their learning. Be amazed. Admire them. You'll be surprised at what they can teach you.

EXERCISES

Model Questioning

Ask more questions of your staff. When presented with a problem of practice, turn it into a question and ask them to do some research within a time limit, in groups—just as in a SOLE session with students. Teachers will own the solution more if they have discovered it themselves.

"What do you think?" is the most powerful pedagogical influence you can have on anyone. I really mean this. I learned this from my school principal, one of the most respected in India, and from my father, India's first Freudian psychoanalyst, in the 1950s.

Also, remember that when you ask a question, you must listen to the answer with every bit of attention and interest you can muster. Pretense of listening and disinterest in listening is the greatest destroyer of trust.

Create Classroom Cohesion

Students and teachers both worry about tests and test scores. If you (and the system) rely only on test scores to evaluate teacher efficacy and student performance, the entire environment of trust and relationship is damaged. Until things change, you, the principal, need to stand between the system and your people. Your students and teachers will appreciate this.

You will have to work out your way to destress the effects of test scores. Here is one possible way.

Take test scores from any test given to a group of students. Give the test itself a score between 0 and 1, based on how good you think the test is for measuring what it is supposed to measure. Call this number G (for goodness of test). For example, if a test of history is measuring only a certain aspect of historical knowledge, you might make $G = 0.6$. We will then assume that each student is not tested for $(1 - G)$ of what was to be measured (i.e., 0.4 in this case). We will then give each student the benefit of the doubt and give him or her the extra score for that part that was not measured. You need to explain this to the students and teachers and, maybe, agree on the value of G together.

Now correct the scores for each student using this process:

$N = N_{max} \times [G \times (S/S_{max}) + (1 - G)]$, where S_{max} is the maximum possible score and S is the actual student score.

For example, if the maximum score is 10 and a student got 7 for a test that you think has a G of 0.6, you would calculate the following:

$N = 10 \times [0.6 \times (7/10) + (1 - 0.6)]$, or $N = 8.2$

In another example, if the maximum score is 15 and a student got 7 for a test you think has a G of 0.8, you would calculate the following:

$N = 15 \times [0.8 \times (7/15) + (1 - 0.8)]$, or $N = 8.6$

These corrected test scores should better reflect your opinion of the test versus student performance. Both students and teachers will take the revised scores more seriously.

Build Collective Teacher Efficacy

Convey your belief in teachers to be effective, and ask them to share their confidence in their students as well. As students (and teachers) experience more success in pursuing learning on their own, they will become more confident in the inevitable outcome—greater learning. Use the method of the grandmother with both students and teachers alike.

CHECKLIST

I believe that trusting in the strengths of people helps build relationships and eventually improves their weaknesses. I can't prove this. You decide.

If you are planning on using any of my suggestions in this chapter, here is how you could test yourself:

☐ Are you focusing more on questions than on answers?

☐ Are you focusing on the present and the future more than the past?

(Continued)

(Continued)

☐ When was the last time you admired your staff and your students for their learning?

☐ Have you collected data on how your school's physical environment encourages or prohibits creativity and collaboration?

The school is like a hive, with a collective of students and a collective of teachers. If you put the strengths of each member of a collective together, then the whole is strong and complete. It does not matter what mistakes any member of the collective makes, the others will always compensate. You can trust that collective and love it. That network of trust and relationship will make the hive a complex and productive structure that no single member of the collective could have built.

You are the leader of that hive. You have balanced the force of learning exactly against the drag of the system. Your school has reached terminal velocity.

You have done your job.

"I FOCUS ON LEARNING AND THE LANGUAGE OF LEARNING"

Jim Knight

VIGNETTE[1]

Before she became an author and senior coaching consultant for the Instructional Coaching Group, Michelle Harris was an instructional coach for the Beaverton School District in Beaverton, Oregon. During that time, Michelle participated in one of our studies of instructional coaching, and one of the coaching partnerships Michelle engaged in for our study was with an outstanding sixth-grade science teacher, Sarah Langston. Michelle frequently told us how impressed she was with Sarah's ability to question and listen to her students, Sarah's commitment to excellence and getting better as a teacher, and especially her deep commitment to the moral purpose of teaching. For Sarah, teaching was an act of social justice.

When Sarah and Michelle partnered together, Sarah had just begun implementing a new science curriculum. The program provided big learning targets, but the targets weren't written in student-friendly language, and they were so general that they didn't communicate what students needed to know, do, and understand. Michelle and Sarah discussed what Sarah might do, and together they decided that they should (a) break down the big targets, (b) use formative evaluation ($d = 0.90$) to see how well students were learning, and (c) then make adjustments so that all students were learning. In conversation with Michelle, Sarah also decided to record her students on video to see how they were experiencing the learning activities in class.

---

[1]This story, drawn from our IES-funded research project conducted in partnership with the Beaverton, Oregon, School District, was first described in *High-Impact Instruction* (Knight, 2013).

Michelle knew a lot about formative evaluation, so she was able to help Sarah break down the learning targets into clear statements that students understood. Michelle and Sarah also decided that Sarah would give students an exit ticket each day to assess who was and was not learning. After that, Sarah would sort student responses into three categories: (a) highly proficient, (b) proficient, and (c) working toward proficient. Michelle and Sarah met frequently to collaboratively explore how Sarah could better meet all students' needs.

On the first day, the assessment results showed that five of the students in Sarah's class were not proficient, so Sarah knew that she had to adjust how students were learning. The problem was that she didn't know what to do. As Michelle told me in an interview, "[Sarah] was stuck right there." To address the needs of all students, including the students who were struggling, Michelle and Sarah collectively decided that Sarah should show students different examples of answers to questions, and then ask students to describe the characteristics of highly proficient answers. The discussions helped students who might not have achieved previously (previous achievement has an effect size of $d = 0.65$) see what success looked like, and they performed much better on future checks for understanding. "The kids," Michelle told us, "who were proficient, the next time, a lot of them became highly proficient . . . and 100% of students became proficient."

Sarah was also able to create a better learning environment for her students by looking at video recordings of her lessons. Michelle recorded Sarah's lesson and shared the video with Sarah. When Sarah watched her students, she realized that none of the eight students in her class who were learning English answered any questions. Quite likely, they didn't answer questions because they were anxious about the challenge of speaking a second language in a room of students who spoke English as their first language.

Sarah met with Michelle to discuss the video, and together they set the goal that all students would participate in at least 70 percent of classroom conversations. Michelle suggested Sarah use the teaching strategy "Talking Tokens," but the strategy didn't have the impact Sarah and Michelle were hoping for. Then Michelle suggested the simple teaching strategy Think–Pair–Share. The result, Michelle told us, was that the students hit the goal. After they started participating, the students who were learning English "sat a little taller, smiled a lot more." That, Michelle said, "had a very positive impact on the community in the classroom." In addition, by working with Michelle and applying some of the factors from this mindframe, Sarah significantly increased her impact on students.

WHAT IS THIS CHAPTER ABOUT?

In Hattie and Zierer's (2018) book *10 Mindframes for Visible Learning: Teaching for Success,* in the mindframe "I focus on learning and the language of learning," the authors describe how prior knowledge and cognitive structures shape the unique ways individual students learn. Additionally, the authors contend that teachers need to assess students' learning situation and guide students' educational experiences in a way that allows for all students to learn. Effective teachers recognize that each student's learning situation is unique and that student thinking and learning develop over time, so they set up learning environments that address students' unique needs so that they can have maximum growth.

The strategies Sarah Langston developed in partnership with Michelle Harris embodied many of the elements of the mindset "a focus on learning and the language of learning." Even though formative evaluation ($d = 0.34$), which Sarah used to assess student learning and adapt her teaching, is not one of the factors described in this chapter, it is the strategy that enabled Sarah to act on many of the factors described here. Through formative evaluation, Sarah and Michelle identified whether or not students were learning, and then Sarah implemented a number of teaching strategies that addressed students' lack of prior knowledge or different levels of development.

In order to help Sarah address the unique needs of all of her students, Michelle took an approach to coaching that also embodied many of the factors in this mindset. Sarah learned socially, in conversation with Michelle, who structured peer-to-peer, dialogical conversations that led to learning for teacher, coach, and most importantly, students. Michelle shared knowledge dialogically to support Sarah's learning when those ideas were needed, and Sarah evolved as her students evolved.

This chapter describes how school leaders who engage in coaching can use the factors in the mindframe "I focus on learning and the language of learning" to support teachers so that they are able to skillfully and artfully respond to students' unique needs by

- providing support so that teachers are able to skillfully and artfully respond to students' needs,

- asking questions that put the focus on students, and

- prioritizing student-focused goals.

WHICH FACTORS FROM THE VISIBLE LEARNING® RESEARCH SUPPORT THIS MINDFRAME?

Jean Piaget's work is one of the main factors Hattie and Zierer (2018) cite for this mindframe (Piagetian programs, d = 1.28). Piaget contended that, over time, the stimuli children experience change how they think, and as children's thinking expands, they learn more.

Piaget also said that the responses learners make to stimuli over time lead learners to develop what he refers to as *cognitive structures*. Once cognitive structures are in place, learners either assimilate new learning into existing structures or experience stimuli that don't fit their structures, and they have to change their thinking. Piaget refers to the conflict that learners experience between stimuli and and cognitive structures as disequilibrium.

For Piaget, learning occurs through disequilibrium, which occurs, as Hattie and Zierer (2018) write, when learners "begin to realize that what they were doing, thinking, and trying to accommodate into their current thinking was discrepant—hence again the mindframe about privileging errors and misunderstandings" (p. 147). Hattie and Zierer state that there is "much support" for programs that account for Piaget's theory of learning, and they cite Shayer and Adey (1981) as one example. The authors contend that learning can be accelerated when (a) learners experience the disequilibrium that arises from cognitive conflict, (b) students learn to take control of their own thinking by being encouraged to be metacognitive, and (c) learning is accelerated through carefully structured conversations with other learners.

Other factors supporting the mindframe include prior achievement (d = 0.65). Students come to class at different starting points, and effective teachers recognize this and use strategies that help different students develop their learning, regardless of their prior achievement. Simply put, students have different prior knowledge and learning experiences and different cognitive structures, so to help students succeed, effective teachers need to assess students and adjust their learning experiences.

WHERE CAN I START?

What we have found after conducting more than twenty years of research on coaching is that there are many ways in which the factors in this mindset come into play during coaching. Coaching is obviously a social learning experience, and the conversations coaches have with teachers should be structured by coaches to meet the unique learning needs of the teacher.

To have learning conversations such as the ones that Michelle and Sarah had, however, certain things need to be in place. Coaching conversations won't happen, for example, where there is an absence of trust. Coaches can build trust through a humble openness to the teachers' perspective, having the best interest of the collaborating teacher at heart, and communicating that we believe in our collaborating teacher. Arrogance, manipulation, and moralistic judgment will always drive out trust.

Coaching also involves a different kind of power relationship than other relationships. A coaching conversation is a conversation between peers, and even administrators who wish to coach need to put on their coaching hat and take off their boss hat when they choose to coach.

Why is this so? First, a mountain of research has shown that telling people what to do is a bad strategy for change (see Knight, 2019). This is especially important since coaching often leads people to question their cognitive structures, which we might also call mental models or mindframes. As Senge (1990) has written, "Mental models are deeply ingrained assumptions, generalizations, or even pictures or images that influence how we understand the world and how we take action" (p. 7), and it is because of mental models that very often "new insights fail to get put into practice because they conflict with deeply held internal images of how the world works, images that limit us to familiar ways of thinking and acting" (p. 163).

Coaching done well, because it surfaces exactly what students are experiencing, may create disequilibrium in teachers. When experience causes teachers to question their mental models, it can be painful, and a coach who talks down to teachers is likely one who will engender resistance. Conversation that cuts to the heart of what we believe about the work we do, work that matters, needs to be safe, trusting, and guided by teachers' perceptions. Telling teachers what they must do might get compliance, but it likely won't change their mental models.

If teachers guide coaching, then how do we ensure that their learning makes a difference for children? This is why goals are so important. If teachers partner with teachers to set goals and then frequently measure students' progress toward goals, learning becomes visible. Such a clear understanding of reality may lead to disequilibrium, so coaches need to be able to help teachers work through times when they don't know what to do, as was the case with Sarah. Simply put, when a coach works from the mindframe "I focus on learning and the language of learning," just like a teacher who works from that mindframe, he or she needs to be able to adapt, respond, and guide as necessary to ensure that teachers and students learn.

CHECKLIST

☐ Teachers will learn more when they learn with someone else who can help them move through challenging learning.

☐ School leaders and coaches should partner with teachers to focus on student learning, not teaching strategies.

☐ School leaders and coaches can turn conversations with teachers toward student learning by asking, "If you implement this teaching strategy, what will be different for students?"

☐ School leaders and coaches shouldn't interfere with teachers' learning, but they should be knowledgeable enough to provide support for learning when it is needed.

☐ School leaders and coaches should help teachers measure student learning frequently (almost daily) to determine whether or not students are learning so that adjustments can be made to how students are learning.

EXERCISES

1. School leaders and coaches who want to build trust (and shouldn't that be everyone?) can learn a lot by keeping a journal of all the times they moralistically judge others. Moralistic judgment is a learning and intimacy killer, so learning how to control it is important for anyone who takes a coaching approach.

2. One of the best ways for school leaders to improve their coaching skills is by video recording themselves during coaching conversations to see how effectively they are coaching. Here are some important things to look for:

   • Who is doing most of the talking?

   • Who is doing most of the thinking and decision making?

   • Am I a good listener—not interrupting, not completing teachers' sentences, not telling them what to do?

   • Am I asking good questions, ones that truly provoke teachers to think, or am I asking questions that are actually advice disguised as a question?

3. Consider creating an instructional playbook (see Knight, Hoffman, Harris, & Thomas, 2020) to deepen your knowledge of teaching practices.

Conclusion

Mindframes: Successful School Leaders' Why

There are many books on school leadership. A search of school leadership books on Amazon.com revealed 20,000+ entries. And, if you are anything like us, you have shelves full of many of these treasured books that have helped to shape your own school leadership beliefs and practices. Many of the books written about school leadership urge readers to adopt a prescribed number of leadership traits, qualities, or skill sets (e.g., create organizations that increase personal capacities; build and sustain a school vision; use data to make instructional decisions; see below the surface, enabling you to detect patterns and their consequences for the system; operate on an open-door policy; be visible; engage in classroom visitations routinely and frequently) in order to be successful. Some of the school leadership books advocate for a specific type of school leader (e.g., change leader, servant leader, leverage leader, transformational leader, instructional leader, resonant leader) to be successful.

Mindframes Actively Shape How We Act

However, there are a very few current books on school leadership that make an attempt to describe how successful school leaders think about the impact of what they do. In our brief review of school leadership books listed on Amazon.com, we found three books whose authors make this effort to some degree. The first is David Loader's (2016) book *The Inner Principal: Reflections on Educational Leadership*. The book is "written from a psychoanalytical perspective. It is concerned with exploring leadership by looking at the inner person, considering the personal qualities of a school leader, her/his vision, beliefs and ways of acting and thinking" (p. 2) that result in school leadership lessons learned over the course of the author's tenure as a principal.

The second book is Alyssa Gallagher and Kami Thordarson's (2018) *Design Thinking for School Leaders: Five Roles and Mindsets That Ignite Positive Change*. The authors argue that school leaders make education better either by operating

105

as "accidental designers" (p. 6) who, at times, unintentionally come upon innovative ideas or solutions to problems they are experiencing, or by being "design-inspired leaders" (p. 6). A design-inspired leader is one who deals with more than just the process or actions, but also grounds her or his actions in five "mindsets that you adopt in your work" (p. 6).

The third book is Simon Sinek's contributions to the idea that how people think about what they do must precede their actions as it provides the context for what they do, which we referenced previously in the introduction, in his books *Start With Why: How Great Leaders Inspire Everyone to Take Action* (Sinek, 2009) and *Find Your Why: A Practical Guide for Discovering Purpose for You and Your Team* (Sinek, Mead, & Docker, 2017). There may well be others, but this gives a sense of the limited number and flavor of the books on leadership thinking.

However, if we widen our review and look for examples of authors with a focus on the values that leaders have that enable them to make sense of the world, which leads to actions, there are at least four authors who have greatly enriched the field of pedagogical, organizational, and leadership literature and could be viewed as among the classics in the field:

- Chris Argyris's and Donald Schön's (1974, 1978) notions that as individuals interact with one another, they "design" their behavior and maintain theories for doing so

- Chris Argyris's (1982) ideas that while people's actions are not always congruent with their "espoused theories" (what they say), they do behave congruently with their mental models (theories in use)

- Peter Senge's (1990) beliefs that our "mental models" are active as they shape how we act

- Viviane Robinson, Margie Hohepa, and Claire Lloyd's (2009) writing about the importance of "theories of action" and making "both the leader's theories and the teachers' theories explicit so that the participants can examine their relative merits and agree whether change is desirable" (p. 129)

The primary aim of our book, similar to the writing of Chris Argyris, Donald Schön, Peter Senge, and Viviane Robinson, is to support their thinking and underscore the idea that for school leaders to make a significant impact on the learning lives of students, they must go beyond their own external behaviors and get at the values that produce these behaviors. Toward that end, we present 10 Mindframes for school leaders. It is our claim that school leaders who develop these ways of thinking are more likely to have major impacts on student learning. A brief overview of these 10 Mindframe chapters follows.

A Brief Overview of the Mindframe Chapters

Chapter 1 considered perhaps the most important of all the mindframes—"I am an evaluator of my impact on teacher/student learning." There is a big difference between a school leader who walks into the schoolhouse and says my main role is to gauge the impact of my leadership practices on student and teacher learning and the school leader who believes their main role is to be a transformational leader, be a believer in values, and manage staff. This means evaluating what we (school leaders) are doing and what the students and teachers are doing, seeing learning through the eyes of students and teachers, and evaluating the effect of our actions on what teachers and their students do *and* the effect of what students and teachers do on what we then need to do. The aim here is for school leaders to use the results of their evaluation of their impact to alter leadership practices "on the fly" while teachers' and school leaders' improvement efforts are going on, with the many students and teachers at various stages of knowing and understanding. Hence, the importance of seeking feedback about the value and magnitude of the leadership decisions. The argument is that school leaders can control the narrative of the school, and a major role of school leaders is to enact the same kind of thinking among the staff and as outlined in *10 Mindframes for Visible Learning: Teaching for Success* (Hattie & Zierer, 2018).

Chapter 2 discussed a corollary way of thinking to the first mindframe—"I see assessment as informing my impact and next steps." As mentioned previously, formative evaluation is one of the primary influences on student learning, and this is the case for the school leader's learning as well. School leaders need feedback about their effects on each student and teacher, hence the notions of assessment as school leader feedback (e.g., the degree of fidelity, quality, adaptation, and dosage of high-probability, school-wide instructional practices, teacher and student perceptions, observational data), school leaders as evaluators, and teacher colleagues and students as peers in the feedback equation. School leaders, like teachers and students, need to debate and agree on where they are going, how they are doing, and where they are going next. In so doing, the collective (i.e., students, teachers, and school leaders) engages in one of the most powerful strategies schools can employ—they "learn about implementation during implementation" (Fullan, 2010, p. 27) and, based on that information, make the necessary next steps.

Chapter 3 presented the idea that highly effective school leaders believe in the value of collaborative teacher efficacy and collective expertise—"I collaborate with my peers and my teachers about my conceptions of progress and my impact." This belief is supported in research from the 1970s by Albert Bandura, a psychologist at Stanford University, who uncovered an interesting pattern in working-group dynamics. He observed that a group's confidence in its abilities seemed to be associated with greater success (Bandura, 1977). In other words, the value a person (e.g., school leader) places in his or her team affects the team's overall performance. Moreover, subsequent research has found this phenomenon to be true across many domains (e.g., Adams & Forsyth, 2006; Goddard et al., 2004). When a school team (e.g., faculty) shares the belief that through their combined ability they can overcome challenges and produce targeted results, groups are more effective (Bandura, 1993).

Chapter 4 underscored the idea that highly successful school leaders see themselves as change agents compared to their less successful counterparts—"I am a change agent and believe all teachers/students can improve." That is, school leaders' role is to change students and teachers from what they are to what they want them to be, what they want them to know and understand. Hattie (2012) states that "this, of course, highlights the moral purposes of education" (p. 162). This mindframe is about school leaders believing that achievement is changeable and is never an immutable or fixed quality; that the role of the school leader is that of an activator, not an impediment to learning; that learning is about challenge; and that attention to social and emotional well-being is critical to engagement, belonging, and achievement in schools. It is also about making certain that both school leaders and teachers see the value of understanding the learning intentions (i.e., school goals/targets) and success criteria (i.e., a breakdown of the learning intention and a benchmark for the quality of learning) as established within the school improvement plan.

Chapter 5—"I strive for challenge rather than merely 'doing my best'"—examined the notion that in most cases, schooling is a complex endeavor filled with challenges— and school leaders must embrace this challenge (e.g., mental models about what students can do, teacher beliefs about pedagogy, and deficit thinking that holds us back from becoming warm demanders of students' cognitive development) and make it the challenge they want it to be. The art of teaching and leading is recognizing that what is challenging to one student or one teacher may not be to another, hence the constant attention to individual differences and seeking the commonality so that peers can work together (e.g., students with their teacher and teachers with teachers and school leaders) to make the difference. School leaders' role is to decide on how to engage students and teachers in the challenge of learning. At the heart of engaging students and teachers in the challenge of learning is school leaders' belief in the importance of clear communications about the learning intentions and success criteria. Why? Because when students and teachers understand these, they can see the purpose of the challenges that are so critical to success in learning.

Chapter 6 reviewed the critical importance that school leaders place on the value of engaging in relentless willingness to examine "what is" against "what we desire" (e.g., effective feedback) and then act on the results of that examination to improve practices—"I give and help students/teachers understand feedback and I interpret and act on feedback given to me." If we have learned anything from the brief overview of the first five chapters, we have come away from that review with an appreciation for the value of feedback that is acted upon. Indeed, the only way to reduce the discrepancy between the school leader's current status and the goal is to provide feedback, seek out information about one's performance, and then interpret and act on the information provided to improve (alter) one's practice.

Chapter 7 considered how important it is that school leaders value the practice of dialogue—"I engage as much in dialogue as in monologue." The research is clear—teachers as well as school leaders talk a lot. According to Yair's (2000) research, teachers talk between 70 and 80 percent of class time. And, if you have ever had the opportunity to experience a faculty meeting at a school, it is perfectly reasonable to assume that school leaders, like teachers, like to hear themselves talk—we have lots of important things to say. While there is a need for teachers and school leaders to impart information, there is a major need for teachers and school leaders to *listen* to students and teachers learning. This listening can come from listening to their questions, their ideas and assumptions, their struggles, their strategies of learning, their successes, their interaction with peers, their outputs, and their views about the learning and the teaching. Another way of saying this is, in dialogue, there is free and creative exploration of complex and subtle issues—a deep "listening" to one another and exposing one's own views, beliefs, and assumptions. Highly effective school leaders understand the value of creating an organization where there is a good balance between imparting information (monologue) and the "deep listening" that is at the heart of dialogue.

Chapter 8 highlighted the belief highly effective school leaders hold that clear communication of goals and what individuals have to do to achieve goal success is essential to learning—"I explicitly inform teachers/students what successful impact looks like from the outset." For adolescent as well as adult learners, it is doubtlessly helpful to know when they have reached the learning goal and the success criteria. Engaging in school improvement efforts in which the success criteria of learning are not touched upon is a lost opportunity. Clearly, there are several ways to reach the learning goal. However, highly successful school leaders understand that the value in revealing the success criteria no later than when the goal is achieved is a recipe for successful and sustained learning in both the classroom and the schoolhouse.

Chapter 9 discussed the conviction that highly successful school leaders hold in putting "people work" ahead of "paper work"—"I build relationships and trust so that learning can occur in a place where it is safe to make mistakes and learn from others." You've certainly heard the real estate agent's mantra, "Location, location, location!" What does this refrain mean? And what possesses real estate agents to repeat it three times? Simply put, it means identical homes can increase or decrease in value due to their location. It's repeated three times for emphasis so you will remember this important investment maxim. It's the number-one rule in real estate, and it's often the most overlooked rule. Similarly, the number-one rule of effective school leaders is relationship, relationship, relationship! Like the previous mantra, it means that similar school leadership practices can be either successful or unsuccessful in their impact based on the quality of relationships between students, teachers, school leaders, and parents. An atmosphere of trust and confidence, safety, care, and goodwill is essential for education in general and student/teacher achievement in particular. This requires student-centered, inspired, and passionate school leaders and teachers who are primarily concerned with students and not with their own knowledge and skills. Hence, the learners (e.g., students, teachers, and school leaders) become the beginning point of the teaching process, and their success becomes the teachers' (i.e., teachers and school leaders) success. The governing mindframe is that teaching and learning are done together, and both sides need one another.

Chapter 10 presented the theory that highly successful school leaders value a focus on learning as opposed to teaching and the prior skills, strategies, and motivation learners (both adolescent as well as adult) bring to the learning—"I focus on learning and the language of learning." In this chapter, the author reinforced prior knowledge and the mental processes that learners use to process and understand information, which shape the unique ways individual students (e.g., students, teachers, and school leaders) learn. He also reinforced how critical it is that teachers (e.g., teachers in the classroom and school leaders within the schoolhouse) assess students' learning situation and guide students' educational experiences in a way that allows for all students to learn. Effective school leaders, like their teacher colleagues, recognize that each student's learning situation is unique and that student thinking and learning develop over time, so they set up learning environments that address students' unique needs so that they can help all achieve beyond what they might have predicted.

VISIBLE LEARNING® Inside

If you are a PC user, you have more than likely seen the label "Intel Inside" affixed on the exterior of your computer or you have specifically shopped for a computer with that label attached. So, what does it stand for? "Intel inside" is a marketing phrase that just means that the computer that displays that phrase in advertisements has an Intel central processing unit inside as opposed to an Advanced Micro Devices processor. In other words, Intel creatively rebranded itself to communicate to its customers that it's the components inside, *their* components inside, a particular product that reflect the true value of the product they are purchasing. Similarly, these 10 Mindframes for school leaders are the essence of creating schools that can claim "Visible Learning® inside." Another way of saying this is that these are the core notions inside a Visible Learning school that communicate the value on which schools need to focus if there is to be success at having major impacts on all students in their learning and achievement. Hence, it is the way school leaders think about their role that makes the difference.

The point is not to suggest to school leaders that they must work their way through a list of ten points, tips, or strategies on the way to becoming a highly effective school leader. Rather, the ideas presented in our book form a complete whole of interdependent and interrelated components. That is, each of these mindframes is mutually dependent (i.e., interdependent) as well as having a reciprocal relation (i.e., interrelated) to one another. For instance, it is impossible for a highly effective school leader to focus only on the most important of all the mindframes ("I am an evaluator of my impact on teacher/student learning") without also routinely collecting assessment data to inform their next steps (e.g., mindframe 2) or collaborating with their peers about their conceptions of progress and impact (i.e., mindframe 3) and giving and helping students and teachers understand feedback at the same time they are interpreting the feedback given to them (i.e., mindframe 6). In this sense, as Hattie and Zierer (2018) suggest, these 10 Mindframes are like the threads that make up a spiderweb. Just as the strength of the spiderweb depends on the resiliency of the threads themselves and on the structure (i.e., the distribution and arrangement) of the threads, the strength of the mindframes web depends on the mindframes themselves and their relationship to one another. In other words, "Every mindframe relates to the others, every mindframe results from the others, every mindframe is in a reciprocal relationship with the others, and every mindframe is supported and strengthened by the others" (p. 163).

Visible School Leaders: Making Improvement Planning Visible

If we were inclined to gaze through the educational looking glass—much like Alice did in Lewis Carroll's 1871 children's literature classic *Through the Looking Glass, and What Alice Found There*—at past school improvement planning research and its connection to student achievement, what would we discover? Would we, for example, find the school improvement planning "glass house" that Alice imagined, filled with beautiful things and nicely connected, or would it be something much different—empty, with little to no connection?

Gazing Through the School Improvement Looking Glass

A positive relationship between school improvement planning, professional practice, and student performance may seem obvious to some. After all, our intuition tells us that high-quality planning should help organizations of all stripes achieve their goals. In other words, the line of reasoning about improvement planning might go something like this: planning compels school leaders and planning teams to develop a "learning agenda" (Boyatzis & McKee, 2005, p. 101) by setting priorities, establishing goals and criteria for success, identifying high-probability strategies, and obtaining commitment from staff. As a result, organizations will be compelled to become more introspective and analytical. They will also develop protocols and procedures for ongoing evaluation and feedback about their policies, priorities, and school-wide practices to see what's working and what's not working. But is that what's really happening during the annual school improvement planning process? What did we find in our gaze through the school improvement looking glass?

To date, there is very little research linking improvement planning to increases in student achievement. For example, Leithwood, Jantzi, and McElheron-Hopkins (2006) conducted a multimethod study that generated and tested a "best evidence" model of school improvement processes (SIP) capable of improving student achievement. One of the conclusions reached by these researchers was that, in general, "the overall effects of our robust SIP model explained a significant amount of the variation in student achievement" (p. 460). More importantly, they discovered that quality implementation of their school improvement plan accounted for the largest effect on student test scores. Key aspects of the quality implementation included such things as "opportunities for staff development, the ability of the school, as a whole, to learn from new ideas and to problem-solve, and collaboration among those in the school" (p. 461). The most surprising finding from this study was that neither the "content of the plan nor the processes used to develop it had any significant effect on at least test score estimates of student learning" (p. 461). This finding seems to say that while the content of the school improvement plan wasn't related to increases in student achievement, the implementation of the content was. Curious indeed.

Unlike the previous study, Kenneth Fernandez (2011) conducted a quantitative study using multivariate regression analysis of 311 school improvement plans within Clark County, Nevada. In this study, he found that "even when controlling for important socioeconomic characteristics of each school, the quality of the SIP was positively related to school improvement (average student growth in NRT score) in math and reading scores and statistically significant" (p. 354). Aside from these two studies, much of the historical literature on the planning process has failed to provide clear or consistent evidence that planning and increases in student achievement have a strong relationship (Armstrong, 1982; Kouzes & Posner, 2012; Phillips & Moutinho, 2000). In some instances, studies have suggested quite the opposite impact: that formal planning can lead to inflexible and myopic practices or, at best, is simply a waste of time and important resources (Bryson & Roering, 1987; Halachmi, 1986; Mintzberg, 1994).

For our purposes, we favor the conclusion from Kenneth Fernandez (2011) that good planning increases the probability that quality teaching combined with effective school leader practices identified within the school improvement plan will lead to increases in learning. This position is certainly illustrated by the Visible Learning® influence "goals": the more clarity teachers have regarding their goals with students' and school leaders' goals with teachers, the more likely learning will be successful;

the more the goals are shared and understood with students and teachers, the greater the likelihood that teachers and students will work toward these goals; and the more teachers succeed in reaching an understanding of the goals with learners and the more school leaders accomplish the same with teachers, the more likely learning will be successful (and enjoyed). This belief alone demonstrates how important quality school improvement planning is.

One last point on school leaders and their work with school improvement efforts. Simon Sinek (2019) believes that "leaders are not responsible for the results; leaders are responsible for the people who are responsible for the results. And the best way to drive performance in an organization is to create an environment in which information can flow freely, mistakes can be highlights and help can be offered and received. In short, an environment in which people feel safe among their own. This is the responsibility of a leader" (p. 129). Just as the mindframes "support and strengthen each other [to] form a coherent structure and thus a stable web together" (Hattie & Zierer, 2018, p. 163), highly effective school leaders have the responsibility to create powerful webs of expertise within the school.

Creating Powerful Webs of Expertise

Educators, much like professionals in the business sector, are increasingly relying on teams as they discover that traditional methods of problem solving, decision making, communication, and implementation are not fast or flexible enough to respond to the ever-increasing challenges of the times. Underscoring this shift, Hattie (2015) believes that "the greatest influence on student progression in learning is having highly expert, inspired and passionate teachers and school leaders working together to maximize the effect of their teaching on all students in their care" (p. 2). School leaders play a major role in this process: to create a powerful web of informed, coordinated effort of expertise in their schools and to lead successful transformations.

The problem with group work, however, is that things always seem to be going wrong when people work together in groups. Many of us find it quicker and easier to "do it myself," thus defeating the cross-contributions and values that derive from working in groups. And even when things are going right, a sharp eye and clearly established criteria for success can often find ways for them to perform a lot better. Pay attention to what's going on inside the group, and school leaders and teachers will undoubtedly see problems there that need fixing.

Everyone within the school (teachers along with school leaders) should be a watchdog over effective collaborative practice. Monitor the team's effectiveness. How can the group make better use of its resources—time, money, processes, and people? Look for what's missing . . . what's getting in the way . . . what needs to happen. Keep an eye on colleagues—who needs encouragement, who's out of line, who's confused, who's using practices that discourage knowledge sharing and information exchange? Conversely, who's engaged in practices that add to the group's collective brain, who's inquiring into the beliefs of their peers or challenging them, and who's challenging each other's practice based on clear standards?

Armed with clearly articulated success criteria (e.g., well-articulated descriptions of proficient collaborative practice), teachers and school leaders can give the group the feedback it needs at the time it needs it the most in order to improve practice. And if group members still see behavior that's hurting performance, have the courage to bring the problem to the rest of the team's attention for corrective action.

One of the best ways to protect the team's results is to find the process problems soon enough to be able to make just-in-time adjustments. Catch them when they are small. Fix them before they have a chance to metastasize or keep team members entrenched in old, unproductive ways of interacting. Even if everyone in your group is competent, committed, and hard-working, group members can't ignore internal problems and still succeed as a team. Outcome is always influenced by approach. Effective teams can't separate the ends from the means. Process will count as much as raw talent in shaping the team's success.

Today's schools are highly complex organizations—often, miniature cities. Highly effective school leaders must be able to leverage accountability and revolutionary technology, implement performance-based evaluation systems proficiently, reengineer outdated management structures, recruit and cultivate nontraditional staff, drive decisions with data (both cause and effect), build professional cultures, and ensure that every child achieves the identified behavioral and academic standards.

To accomplish these expectations, school leaders must make certain that everyone has easy access to the organization's expertise, its collective brain. Answers need to come from the best-informed people, who typically are closest to the action—the implementation. Everyone within the organization needs to be sufficiently linked so they know where they are in relation to the organization's goals, expected practices, and what next steps to take for themselves. A highly integrated system such as this operates only when there is a tight web of informed, coordinated effort.

How do school leaders pull this off? Certainly not by being the head honcho, the one with all the answers. Rather, you privilege others by empowering all within the organization. You make it easy for everyone to connect with each other, resolve problems at their level, generate ideas, and make and learn from mistakes. Highly skilled school leaders hook people up in order to link the accounting of their own teaching/leading to its actual or probable impact on students. That is, they activate and scale collaborative expertise by orchestrating opportunities for teachers and school leaders to come together and to reflect and act on their reflection in order to significantly impact the learning lives of those students entrusted to their care.

Highly Effective School Leaders Are to "DIIE" For

Let's return for a moment to the research findings from Leithwood et al. (2006). Recall that they discovered, among other things, that quality implementation of their school improvement plan accounted for the largest effect on student test scores. That is, improvement in student learning is a by-product of implementation done well. However, there is consensus from the research that most programs in schools are generally not implemented well (Dusenbury, Brannigan, Hansen, Walsh, & Falco, 2005). So, what specifically would highly effective school leaders be doing if they are doing implementation well?

Recall in the introduction that we introduced the idea that "school leaders are to DIIE for!," that is, school leaders need to be expert at Diagnosis, Interventions, Implementation, and Evaluation. To be expert at implementation, school leaders must demonstrate the ability to address four related factors: fidelity, dosage, adaptation, and quality of delivery. *Fidelity* is considered the procedural adherence to the structure and sequence of activities outlined by a program theory or plan of action (Domitrovich, Gest, Jones, Gill, & Sanford Derousie, 2010). For example, say you were interested in developing a feedback culture within your school such that the feedback practices between teachers and students, or students and students, or teachers and teachers, or school leaders and teachers are implemented according to how the research describes the quality practices associated with the particular intervention. Thus, your first step is to determine what the research says constitutes quality feedback. Toward that end, going back to our earlier example, you will probably want to pay attention to feedback practices that

- include three components: what was done well (according to the success criteria), what needs improvement (based on the success criteria), and what are the specific "where to next" suggestions (based on the success criteria);

- relate to the learning goal(s), which were shared and clarified with students and teachers at the outset of the learning cycle; and

- are focused on the product or task, the processes used, or the learner's self-regulation, not on the learner as a person.

Adaptation is described as any alteration of the specific program components or the process in delivery, for instance, changing the language in a reading program to suit the specific context. If we return to the aforementioned example of feedback, in some cases we have encountered schools using the term *scales* in place of success criteria. So, an adaptation like that makes a great deal of sense. *Dosage* is a specific measurement of amount regardless of circumstances. It considers the amount of exposure to the intervention being implemented in terms of both completeness (e.g., dosage delivered) and exposure (e.g., dosage received), such as the total percentage of feedback provided or delivered on effective feedback practices. *Quality,* in this case, refers to the quality of the actual delivery (i.e, feedback); it is an assessment to determine whether the process of delivery was as expected according to the developer's expectations (e.g., the established success criteria). For example, when teachers provide feedback to students or when school leaders provide teachers feedback, that feedback is delivered as expected (i.e., according to the success criteria). Another way of saying this is that, armed with what the research says constitutes "fidelity" (see previous bullet points), highly effective school leaders will work with teachers to develop a school-wide implementation rubric that guides both teachers' and school leaders' practices, self-reflection, and observational feedback (against the success criteria within the implementation rubric) as they work to measure the fidelity of implementation (Domitrovich et al., 2010). Moreover, Domitrovich et al. (2010) posit that "implementation quality is the cornerstone of the dissemination process" (p. 294). All of this addresses the question "What specifically would highly effective school leaders be doing if they are doing implementation well?"

A "Just Cause" for Schooling

As Simon Sinek (2019) claims, a "Just Cause" is a specific vision about the future that does not yet exist, a future state so appealing that people are willing to make sacrifices in order to help advance toward that vision. Our notion of the Just Cause for schooling is for school leaders and teachers to create a learning environment where children want to come to learn, want to invest in learning, enjoy the mastery of learning, and are invited to reinvest in learning. We want schools to be places where children are taught precious knowledge, heritages of themselves and others, respect for self and others, and how to participate in the rule of law and fundamental premises of a democracy. We desire for schools to be inviting places where children want to explore, create, be curious, and relate and transfer ideas, as these are the very attributes we would want them to explore and exhibit when they are adults.

School leaders along with teachers do not create the future for children, they are creating their future now; they will critique, overturn current thinking, and create new futures. Our role is not to train people, equip students with skill sets, or in any way ask them to fit right into things as they are. We need moral outrage, compassion, and courage with the aim of collectively making goodness more reliable and sought after. We believe the best way to do the above is to create an environment in which information can flow freely, mistakes can be comfortably made, and teaching can be offered and received in a way all students feel safe.

Our notion of the Just Cause for schooling is rooted in our deep desire for children to enjoy childhood as that is among the best predictors of learning how to enjoy being an adult and citizen.

References

Adams, C. M., & Forsyth, P. B. (2006). Proximate sources of collective teacher efficacy. *Journal of Educational Administration, 44*(6), 625–642.

Archibald, T., Sharrock, G., Buckley, J., & Cook, N. (2016). Assumptions, conjectures, and other miracles: The application of evaluative thinking to theory of change models in community development. *Evaluation and Program Planning, 59,* 119–127.

Argyris, C. (1982). *Learning and action: Individual and organizational.* San Francisco: Jossey-Bass.

Argyris, C., & Schön, D. A. (1974). *Theory in practice: Increasing professional effectiveness.* San Francisco: Jossey-Bass.

Argyris, C., & Schön, D. A. (1978). *Organizational learning: A theory of action perspective.* London: Addison-Wesley.

Armstrong, J. S. (1982). The value of formal planning for strategic decisions: Review of empirical research. *Strategic Management Journal, 3,* 197–211.

Ausubel, D. P. (1968). *Educational psychology: A cognitive view.* New York: Holt, Rinehart & Winston.

Baker, A., & Bruner, B. (2012). *Integrating evaluative capacity into organizational practice.* Cambridge, MA: Bruner Foundation. Retrieved from www.evaluativethinking.org/docs/Integ_Eval_Capacity_Final.pdf

Bandura, A. (1977). Toward a unifying theory of behavioral change. *Psychological Review, 84*(2), 191–215.

Bandura, A. (1986). *Social foundations of thought and action: A social cognitive theory.* Englewood Cliffs, NJ: Prentice-Hall.

Bandura, A. (1993). Perceived self-efficacy in cognitive development and functioning. *Educational Psychologist, 28*(2), 117–148.

Bandura, A. (1998). Personal and collective efficacy in human adaptation and change. In J. G. Adair, D. Bélanger, & K. L. Dion (Eds.), *Advances in psychological science, Volume 1: Social, personal, and cultural aspects* (pp. 51–71). Hove, UK: Psychology Press.

Bandura, A. (2000). Exercise of human agency through collective efficacy. *Current Directions in Psychological Science, 9*(3), 75–78.

Bloom, B. S. (1968). Learning for mastery. *Evaluation Comment (UCLA-CSEIP), 1*(2), 1–12.

Bloom, B. S. (1971). Mastery learning. In J. H. Block (Ed.), *Mastery learning: Theory and practice* (pp. 47–63). New York: Holt, Rinehart and Winston.

Bloom, H. S., Hill, C. J., Black, A. R., & Lipsey, M. W. (2008). Performance trajectories and performance gaps as achievement effect-size benchmarks for educational interventions. *Journal of Research on Educational Effectiveness, 1*(4), 289–328.

Boyatzis, R., & McKee, A. (2005). *Resonant leadership.* Boston: Harvard Business.

Bryson, J., & Roering, W. D. (1987). Applying private-sector strategic planning in the public sector. *Journal of the American Planning Association, 53,* 9–22.

Bulris, M. E. (2009). *A meta-analysis of research on the mediated effects of principal leadership on student achievement: Examining the effect size of school culture on student achievement as an indicator of teacher effectiveness* (Unpublished doctoral dissertation). East Carolina University, Greenville, North Carolina.

Cavanaugh, A. (2016). *Contagious culture: Show up, set the tone, and intentionally create an organization that thrives.* New York: McGraw-Hill Education.

Cohen, J., McCabe, E. M., Michelli, M. M., & Pickeral, T. (2009). School climate: Research, policy, practice, and teacher education. *Teachers College Record, 111,* 180–213.

Domitrovich, C. E., Gest, S. D., Jones, D., Gill, S., & Sanford Derousie, R. M. (2010). Implementation quality: Lessons learned in the context of the Head Start REDI trial. *Early Childhood Research Quarterly, 25,* 284–298.

Donohoo, J., Hattie, J., & Eells, R. (2018). The power of collective efficacy. *Educational Leadership, 75*(6), 41–44.

Donohoo, J., & Katz, S. (2020). *Quality implementation: Leveraging collective efficacy to make "what works" actually work.* Thousand Oaks, CA: Corwin.

Dusenbury, L., Brannigan, R., Hansen, W. B., Walsh, J., & Falco, M. (2005). Quality of implementation: Developing measures crucial to understanding the diffusion of preventive interventions. *Health Education Research, 20*(3), 308–313.

Fernandez, K. E. (2011). Evaluating school improvement plans and their affect on academic performance. *Educational Policy, 25*(2), 338–367.

Fisher, D., Frey, N., Almarode, J., Flories, K., & Nagel, D. (2020). *The PLC+ playbook: A hands-on guide to collectively improving student learning grades K–12.* Thousand Oaks, CA: Corwin.

Fisher, D., Smith, D., & Frey, N. (2020). *Teacher credibility and collective efficacy.* Thousand Oaks, CA: Corwin.

Fullan, M. (2009). *The challenge of change: Start school improvement now!* Thousand Oaks, CA: Corwin.

Fullan, M. (2010). *Motion leadership: The skinny on becoming change savvy.* Thousand Oaks, CA: Corwin.

Fullan, M. (2014). *The principal: Three keys to maximizing impact.* San Francisco: Jossey-Bass.

Fullan, M. (2015). *The new meaning of educational change* (5th ed.). New York: Teachers College Press.

Fullan, M. (2019). *Nuance: Why some leaders succeed and others fail.* Thousand Oaks, CA: Corwin.

Fullan, M., Quinn, J., & Adam, E. (2016). *The taking action guide to building coherence in schools, districts, and systems.* Thousand Oaks, CA: Corwin.

Fullan, M., Quinn, J., & McEachen, J. (2018). *Deep learning: Engage the world change the world.* Thousand Oaks, CA: Corwin.

Fullan, M., & Rincon-Gallardo, S. (2016). Developing high-quality public education in Canada: The case of Ontario. In F. Adamson, B. Astrand, & L. Darling-Hammond (Eds.), *Global education reform: How privatization and public investment influence education outcomes* (pp. 169–193). New York: Routledge.

Funnell, S. C. (2000). Developing and using a program theory matrix for program evaluation and performance monitoring. *New Directions for Evaluation, 2000*(87), 91–101.

Gallagher, A., & Thordarson, K. (2018). *Design thinking for school leaders: Five roles and mindsets that ignite positive change.* Alexandria, VA: ASCD

Garmston, R., & Wellman, B. (1999). *The adaptive school: A sourcebook for developing collaborative groups.* Norwood, MA: Christopher Gordon Publishers.

Goddard, R. D. (2001). Collective efficacy: A neglected construct in the study of schools and student achievement. *Journal of Educational Psychology, 93*(3), 467–476.

Goddard, R. D., Goddard, Y., Kim, E. S., & Miller, R. (2015). A theoretical and empirical analysis of the roles of instructional leadership, teacher collaboration, and collective efficacy beliefs in support of student learning. *American Journal of Education, 121*, 501–530.

Goddard, R. D., Hoy, W. K., & Woolfolk Hoy, A. (2004). Collective efficacy beliefs: Theoretical developments, empirical evidence, and future directions. *Educational Researcher, 33*(3), 3–13.

Gully, S., Incalcaterra, K., Joshi, A., & Beaubein, J. M. (2002). A meta-analysis of team-efficacy, potency, and performance: Interdependence and level of analysis as moderators of observed relationships. *Journal of Applied Psychology, 87*(5), 819–832.

Guskey, T. R. (2010). Lessons of mastery learning. *Educational Leadership, 68*(2), 52–57.

Guskey, T. R., & Link, L. J. (2019). The forgotten element of instructional leadership: Grading. *Educational Leadership, 76*(6). Retrieved from http://www.ascd.org/publications/educational-leadership/mar19/vol76/num06/The-Forgotten-Element-of-Instructional-Leadership@-Grading.aspx

Halachmi, A. (1986). Strategic planning and management: Not necessarily. *Public Productivity Review, 40*, 35–50.

Hargreaves, A., & Fullan, M. (2012). *Professional capital: Transforming teaching in every school.* New York: Teachers College Press.

Harlen, W. (2007). *Assessment of learning.* London: Sage.

Hattie, J. (2009). *Visible Learning: A synthesis of over 800 meta-analyses relating to achievement.* New York: Routledge.

Hattie, J. (2012). *Visible Learning for teachers: Maximizing impact on learning.* New York: Routledge.

Hattie, J. (2015). *What works best: The politics of collaborative expertise.* New York: Pearson.

Hattie, J. (2019). *Visible Learning: 250+ influences on student achievement.* Thousand Oaks, CA: Corwin.

Hattie, J., & Timperley, H. (2007). The power of feedback. *Review of Educational Research, 77*(1), 81–112.

Hattie, J., & Zierer, K. (2018). *10 mindframes for Visible Learning: Teaching for success.* London: Routledge.

Hattie, J. A., & Donoghue, G. M. (2016). Learning strategies: A synthesis and conceptual model. *NPJ Science of Learning, 1,* 16013. Retrieved from https://www.nature.com/articles/npjscilearn201613

Hendriks, M. A., Scheerens, J., & Sleegers, P. (2014). Effects of evaluation and assessment on student achievement: A review and meta-analysis. In M. A. Hendriks, *The influence of school size, leadership, evaluation, and time on student outcomes* (pp. 127-174). Enschede, The Netherlands: University of Twente.

Illeris, K. (2015). The development of a comprehensive and coherent theory of learning. *European Journal of Education, 50*(1), 29–40.

Isoré, M. (2009). *Teacher evaluation: Current practices in OECD countries and a literature review* (OECD Education Working Papers No. 23). Retrieved from https://read.oecd-ilibrary.org/education/teacher-evaluation-current-practices-in-oecd-countries-and-a-literature-review_223283631428#page1

Kingston, N. M., & Nash, B. (2011). Formative assessment: A meta-analysis and a call for research. *Educational Measurement: Issues and Practice, 30*(4), 28–37.

Kingston, N. M., & Nash, B. (2015). Erratum. *Educational Measurement: Issues and Practice, 34*(1), 55.

Kluger, A. N., & DeNisi, A. (1996). The effects of feedback interventions on performance: A historical review, a meta-analysis, and a preliminary feedback intervention theory. *Psychological Bulletin, 119*(2), 254–284.

Knight, J. (2007). *Instructional coaching: A partnership approach to improving instruction.* Thousand Oaks, CA: Corwin.

Knight, J. (2013). *High-impact instruction: A framework for great teaching.* Thousand Oaks, CA: Corwin.

Knight, J. (2019). Why teacher autonomy is central to coaching success. *Educational Leadership, 77*(3), 14–20.

Knight, J., Hoffman, A., Harris, M., & Thomas, S. (2020). *The instructional playbook: The missing link for translating research into practice.* Lawrence, KS: One Fine Bird Press.

Kouzes, J. M., & Posner, B. Z. (2012). *The leadership challenge: How to make extraordinary things happen in organizations* (5th ed.). San Francisco: Jossey-Bass.

Leahy, S., Lyon, C., Thompson, M., & Wiliam, D. (2005). Classroom assessment: Minute-by-minute and day-by-day. *Educational Leadership, 63*(3), 18–24.

Leahy, S., & Wiliam, D. (2009). *Embedding formative assessment.* London: Specialist Schools and Academies Trust.

Leithwood, K., & Jantzi, D. (2008). Linking leadership to student learning: The contributions of leader efficacy. *Educational Administration Quarterly, 44*(4), 496–528.

Leithwood, K., Jantzi, D., & McElheron-Hopkins, C. (2006). The development and testing of a school improvement model. *School Effectiveness and School Improvement, 17*(4), 441–464. doi: 10.1080/09243450600743533

Leithwood, K., Louis, K. S., Anderson, S., & Wahlstrom, K. (2004). *How leadership influences student learning.* New York: The Wallace Foundation.

Leithwood, K., Strauss, T., & Anderson, S. (2007). District contributions to school leaders' sense of efficacy: A qualitative analysis. *Journal of School Leadership, 17*(6), 735–770.

Link, L. J. (2018). Finding expertise in your own backyard: K–12 educators collaborate with a nearby university to devise a strategy that serves both partners' needs and interests. *School Administrator, 10*(75), 38–42.

Link, L. J. (2019). Leadership in grading reform. In T. R. Guskey & S. M. Brookhart (Eds.), *What we know about grading: What works, what doesn't, and what's next?* (pp. 157–194). Alexandria, VA: ASCD.

Little, J. W. (1990). The persistence of privacy: Autonomy and initiative in teachers' professional relations. *Teachers College Record, 91*(4), 509–536.

Loader, D. (2016). *The inner principal: Reflections on educational leadership.* Torrance, CA: Constructing Modern Knowledge Press.

Locke, E., & Latham, G. (1990). *A theory of goal setting and task performance.* Englewood Cliffs, NJ: Prentice-Hall.

Locke, E., & Latham, G. (2006). New directions in goal-setting theory. *Current Directions in Psychological Science, 15*(5), 265–268.

Lortie, D. (1975). *School teacher: A sociological study.* Chicago: University of Chicago Press.

Manna, P. (2015). *Developing excellent school principals to advance teaching and learning: Considerations for state policy.* New York: The Wallace Foundation.

Marzano, R., Waters, T., & McNulty, B. (2005). *School leadership that works: From research to results.* Alexandria, VA: Association for Supervision and Curriculum Development.

Marzano, R. J. (2012). The two purposes of teacher evaluation. *Educational Leadership, 70*(3), 14–19.

Marzano, R. J., Gaddy, B. B., Foseid, M. C., Foseid, M. P., & Marzano, J. S. (2005). *A handbook for classroom management that works.* Alexandria, VA: ASCD.

Mielke, P., & Frontier, T. (2012). Keeping improvement in mind. *Educational Leadership, 70*(3), 10–13.

Mintzberg, H. (1994). *The rise and fall of strategic planning.* New York: Free Press.

Noguera, P. (2008). *The trouble with black boys . . . and other reflections on race, equity, and the future of public education.* San Francisco: Jossey-Bass.

Nystrand, M. (1990). Sharing words: The effects of readers on developing writers. *Written Communication, 7*(1), 3–24.

Nystrand, M., & Gamoran, A. (1991). Instructional discourse, student engagement, and literature achievement. *Research in the Teaching of English, 25*(3), 261–290.

Nystrand, M., Wu, L. L., Gamoran, A., Zeiser, S., & Long, D. A. (2003). Questions in time: Investigating the structure and dynamics of unfolding classroom discourse. *Discourse Processes, 35*(2), 135–198.

Papay, J. P., & Kraft, M. A. (2016). The myth of the performance plateau. *Educational Leadership, 73*(8), 36–42.

Perry, A. (1908). *The management of a city school.* New York: Macmillan.

Phillips, P. A., & Moutinho, L. (2000). The strategic planning index: A tool for measuring strategic planning effectiveness. *Journal of Travel Research, 38,* 369–379.

Pollock, M. (2017). *SchoolTalk: Rethinking what we say about and to students every day.* New York: New Press.

Popper, K. R. (1959). *The logic of scientific discovery.* New York: Routledge.

Quinn, J., McEachen, J., Fullan, M., Gardner, M., & Drummy, M. (2020). *Dive into deep learning: Tools of engagement.* Thousand Oaks, CA: Corwin.

Ramos, M., Silva, S., Pontes, F., Fernandez, A., & Nina, K. (2014). Collective teacher efficacy beliefs: A critical review of the literature. *International Journal of Humanities and Social Science, 4*(7), 179–188.

Redfield, D. L., & Rousseau, E. W. (1981). A meta-analysis of experimental research on teacher questioning behavior. *Review of Educational Research, 51*(2), 237–245.

Robinson, V. (2009). *Open-to-learning conversations: Background paper. Module 3: Building Trust in Schools Through Open-to-learning Conversations.* First-time Principals Programme. The University of Auckland: NZ.

Robinson, V., Hohepa, M., & Lloyd, C. (2009). *School leadership and student outcomes: Identifying what works and why: Best evidence synthesis iteration [BES].* Auckland, New Zealand: Ministry of Education.

Robinson, V. M. J., Lloyd, C. A., & Rowe, K. J. (2008). The impact of leadership on student outcomes: An analysis of the differential effects of leadership types. *Educational Administration Quarterly, 44*(5), 635–674.

Ruiz-Primo, M. A., & Li, M. (2013). Examining formative feedback in the classroom context: New research perspectives. In J. H. McMillan (Ed.), *Sage handbook of research on classroom assessment* (2nd ed., pp. 215–232). Thousand Oaks, CA: Sage.

Sanders, M. (2014). Principal leadership for school, family, and community partnerships: The role of a systems approach to reform implementation. *American Journal of Education, 120*(2), 233–255.

Sandoval, J., Challoo, L., & Kupczynski, L. (2011). The relationship between teachers' collective efficacy and student achievement at economically disadvantaged middle school campuses. *Journal on Educational Psychology, 5*(1), 9–23.

Saphier, J. (2017). The principal's role in high expectations of teachers. *Principal, 96*(3), 8–11.

Scriven, M. (1967). The methodology of evaluation. In R. W. Tyler, R. M. Gagné, & M. Scriven (Eds.), *Perspectives of curriculum evaluation* (pp. 39–83). AERA Monograph Series on Curriculum Evaluation, 1. Chicago: Rand McNally.

Scriven, M. (1991a). Beyond formative and summative evaluation. In M. W. McLaughlin & D. C. Phillips (Eds.), *Evaluation and education at quarter century* (90th yearbook of the National Society for the Study of Education, pp. 18–64). Chicago: University of Chicago Press.

Scriven, M. (1991b). *Evaluation thesaurus.* Newbury Park, CA: Sage.

Seijts, G., & Latham, G. (2005). Learning versus performance goals: When should each be used? *Academy of Management Executive, 19*(1), 124–131.

Senge, P. M. (1990). *The fifth discipline: The art and practice of the learning organization.* New York: Doubleday.

Shaw, D. (2017). Accomplished teaching: Using video recorded micro-teaching discourse to build candidate teaching competencies. *Journal of Interactive Learning Research, 28*(2), 161–180.

Shayer, M., & Adey, P. (1981). *Towards a science of science teaching: Cognitive development and curriculum demand.* London: Heinemann.

Sinek, S. (2009). *Start with why: How great leaders inspire everyone to take action.* New York: Penguin Random House.

Sinek, S. (2019). *The infinite game.* New York: Penguin Random House.

Sinek, S., Mead, D., & Docker, P. (2017). *Find your why: A practical guide for discovering purpose for you and your team.* New York: Penguin Random House.

Slavin, R. E., Hurley, E. A., & Chamberlain, A. M. (2003). Cooperative learning and achievement. In W. M. Reynolds & G. J. Miller (Eds.), *Handbook of psychology: Volume 7: Educational psychology* (pp. 177–198). Hoboken, NJ: Wiley.

Smith, K. (2018). *Clarity first.* New York: McGraw-Hill.

Speckesser, S., Runge, J., Foliano, F., Bursnall, M., Hudson-Sharp, N., Rolfe, H., & Anders, J. (2018). *Embedding Formative Assessment: Evaluation report and executive summary.* London: Education Endowment Foundation.

Stone, D., & Heen, S. (2014). *Thanks for the feedback: The science and art of receiving feedback well.* New York: Penguin.

Sue, D. W., Bucceri, J., Lin, A. I., Nadal, K. L., & Torino, G. C. (2007). Racial microaggressions and the Asian American experience. *Cultural Diversity and Ethnic Minority Psychology, 13*(1), 72–81.

Suftka, K. J., & George, M. D. (2000). Setting clear and mutual expectations. *Liberal Education, 86*(1), 48–54.

Thapa, A., Cohen, J., Guffy, S., & Higgins-D'Alessandro, A. (2013). A review of school climate research. *Review of Educational Research, 83,* 357–385.

Tomlinson, C. A. (2006). An alternative to ability grouping. *Principal Leadership, 6*(8), 31–32.

Tschannen-Moran, M. (2014). *Trust matters: Leadership for successful schools* (2nd ed.). San Francisco: Jossey-Bass.

Tschannen-Moran, M., Woolfolk Hoy, A., & Hoy, W. K. (1998). Teacher efficacy: Its meaning and measure. *Review of Educational Research, 68*(2), 202–248.

Tuytens, M., & Devos, G. (2016). The role of feedback from the school leader during teacher evaluation for teacher and school improvement. *Teachers and Teaching, 23*(1), 6–24.

Wahlstrom, K., & Louis, K. S. (2008). How teachers experience principal leadership: The roles of professional community, trust, efficacy, and shared responsibility. *Educational Administration Quarterly, 44*(4), 458–495.

Welch, J., & Hodge, M. (2017). Assessing impact: The role of leadership competency models in developing effective school leaders. *School Leadership & Management, 38*(4), 355–377.

Wiggins, G. (2012). Seven keys to effective feedback. *Educational Leadership, 70*(1), 10–16.

Woolley, A. W., Chabris, C. F., Pentland, A., Hashmi, N., & Malone, T. W. (2010). Evidence for a collective intelligence factor in the performance of human groups. *Science, 330,* 686–688.

Yair, G. (2000). Educational battlefields in America: The tug-of-war over students' engagement with instruction. *Sociology of Education, 73*(4), 247–269.

Index

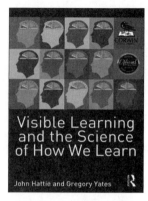

10 MINDFRAMES FOR VISIBLE LEARNING

10 MINDFRAMES FOR LEADERS

VISIBLE LEARNING FEEDBACK

DEVELOPING ASSESSMENT-CAPABLE VISIBLE LEARNERS, Grades K–12

VISIBLE LEARNING FOR LITERACY, Grades K–12

TEACHING LITERACY IN THE VISIBLE LEARNING CLASSROOM, Grades K–5, 6–12

VISIBLE LEARNING FOR MATHEMATICS, Grades K–12

TEACHING MATHEMATICS IN THE VISIBLE LEARNING CLASSROOM, Grades K–2, 3–5, 6–8, & High School

VISIBLE LEARNING FOR SCIENCE, Grades K–12

VISIBLE LEARNING FOR SOCIAL STUDIES, Grades K–12

A SAGE Publishing Company

Helping educators make the greatest impact

CORWIN HAS ONE MISSION: to enhance education through intentional professional learning.

We build long-term relationships with our authors, educators, clients, and associations who partner with us to develop and continuously improve the best evidence-based practices that establish and support lifelong learning.